THE ROMANCE OF
DOUBLE WEDDING RING
QUILTS

THE PATCHWORK BOOK

The Woman's World Service Library

THE ROMANCE OF DOUBLE WEDDING RING QUILTS

Robert Bishop

Patterns and Instructions by
Carter Houck

E.P. DUTTON   NEW YORK

In association with the
MUSEUM OF AMERICAN FOLK ART   NEW YORK

These three pillows have covers in the Double Wedding Ring design.

Book design and line art by Marilyn Rey

This book is dedicated to
Cuesta Benberry
eminent quilt historian
and gracious lady

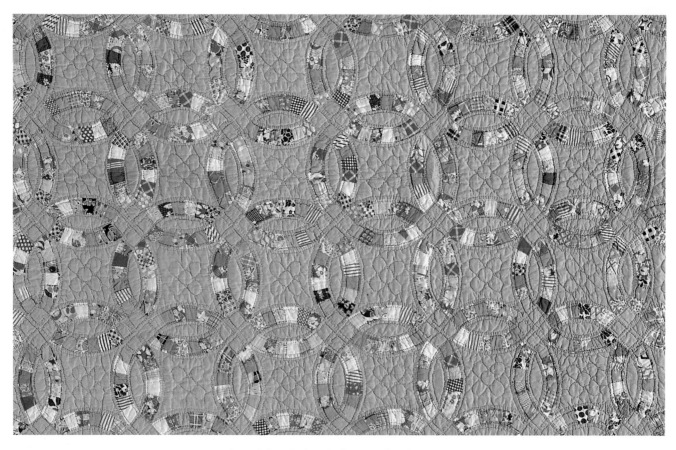

Enlarged detail of quilt illustrated in figure 17.

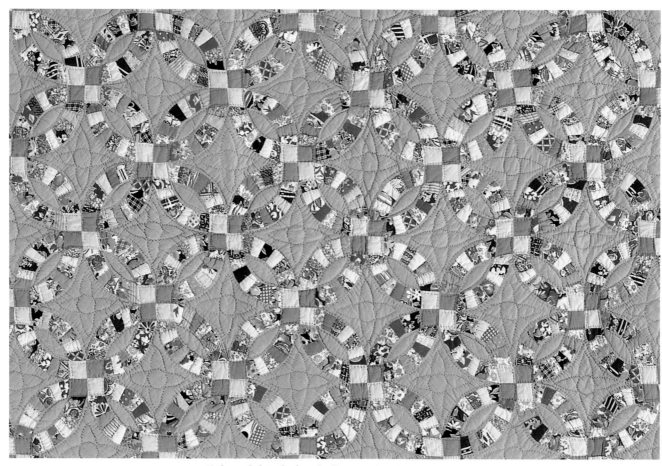

Enlarged detail of quilt illustrated in figure 62.

CONTENTS

1. Candlewick coverlet. Dated June 1897. 78″ x 66″. In this very unusual piece the Double Wedding Ring design is worked in candlewicking. The background material was woven in two panels, and the piece is embroidered with the date "June 1897." Candlewick quilt blocks were offered in several publicatons in the late 1920s and 1930s. The earliest published pattern that has been found was offered for sale by William Pinch of Cleveland, Ohio, in 1928.

PREFACE

This book and the exhibition organized by the Museum of American Folk Art, New York City, that inspired it grew out of a personal experience.

About three years ago I purchased a remarkable Double Wedding Ring quilt with a red background at an Atlanta antiques show. When I first saw this handsome bedcover, the bold design, vibrant colors, and impressive quilting abilities of its skillful maker caused me to pause and examine it carefully. The quilt was marked "$850.00." The dealer explained, "I've had the quilt a long time. You are the first person who has even asked the price." When I hesitated he continued, "I don't handle quilts. You can have it for what I paid for it." I promptly wrote him a check for the $250.00 he requested and carried my treasure home.

As with many collectors, my personal lifestyle does not easily accommodate the addition of a quilt. I first tried it on a painted and decorated cannonball bed from the 1830s. Almost immediately my Doberman and two Manchester Terriers assumed a contented position directly in the center of it.

Next, I had the quilt mounted on stretchers so that it could be hung. After spending nearly $200.00 in preparation, I discovered that it was simply too large and the design too dominant to fit into the decorative scheme of my house. Defeated? Yes. I sadly folded this Southern beauty and tucked it away in the back of my closet.

Over the next several months, I continued to see additional Double Wedding Ring quilts at antiques shows and flea markets. Each time, I stopped to look and queried the dealer about the quilt's origins—who made it, when, and where. Colorful pieces that were well-crafted and graphically dramatic were the most expensive. Conventional examples that had been used extensively, washed excessively, or needed repair were of little interest.

As I continued to discover additional Double Wedding Ring quilts in the marketplace, my curiosity increased. What struck me most was that unique bedcovers could result from countless women working with the same design. I developed a deep curiosity, and in time it became important to learn about the origins of the Double Wedding Ring pattern and to try to document fully its use by American needlewomen.

A body of information evolved. Many quilt scholars believe that the pattern emerged after the Civil War. The earliest documented textile in the Double Wedding Ring design to surface, however, is an embroidered candlewick bedspread that is initialed "H.L." and dated "June 1897" (fig. 1). In the late 1920s, popular farm magazines began to illustrate the pattern and to offer readers mail-order quilt kits. Most of the quilts remaining today are stitched from fabrics that can be dated from the 1930s and 1940s. It seems certain that the pattern reached its zenith in rural America during the Depression; slightly later it was borrowed by Amish women in Pennsylvania, Ohio, and Indiana. Today, Amish Double Wedding Ring quilts with black backgrounds are the most prized.

I have discovered an endless variety of Double Wedding Ring types. Some are pieced; some are appliquéd; others are embroidered. Some are stitched using the traditional block technique, while still others are to be most admired for their extraordinary quilting.

I consider this book a study of American creativity. Working with a prescribed pattern, rural women of the early 20th century fashioned practical and beautiful works of art for family use. At the same time, they created a textile legacy for themselves and for future generations.

ROBERT BISHOP

Enlarged detail of quilt illustrated in figure 34.

INTRODUCTION

For over a decade enthusiasts and scholars have attempted to discover the origins of the very popular quilt pattern known as Double Wedding Ring. Bonnie Leman, founder and editor-in-chief of *Quilter's Newsletter Magazine*, in the June 1978 issue sparked a heated debate with the article, "The Great American Quilt Classics: Double Wedding Ring." The article, historical in content, attempted to trace the development of the design. "A good whodunit is always interesting, and quilt buffs have been trying to unravel the thread of the Double Wedding Ring story for years. It is possibly the most often made pieced pattern in the entire repertoire of American quiltmakers. It is such a familiar design that in the minds of many people it is *the* patchwork quilt. Out of the thousands of quilt designs in existence, this is one of the few that could stand alone as an instantly recognizable symbol of American patchwork. Yet, there is hardly anything in print about the history and origin of this design. It has been largely ignored by quilt historians, probably because none of them has been able to find out for sure when or where the design was created—or by whom. There aren't even folk tales about it to satisfy our curiosity.

"Ruth Finley, who relates so beautifully the story behind dozens of other designs in *Old Patchwork Quilts*, says nothing at all. The Orlofskys in another good reference, *Quilts in Americca*, say, 'Late in the [19th] century a pattern known as the "Double Wedding Ring" became popular, and has remained so to this day, but without much symbolic significance....' Carrie Hall (*The Romance of the Patchwork Quilt in America*) tells us, 'Real quilt enthusiasts delight in this all-over pattern, but it is hardly the design for the novice to undertake.' Delores Hinson reports in *The Quilting Manual* that the earliest ones were made in the 1870s or 1880s.

"Although facts about the design elude us, it is likely that it began to be a big favorite in the Depression period of the '20s and '30s, because it is essentially a scrap quilt—the only kind most people could afford to make in those lean days—yet it was a scrap quilt with a joyful and romantic connotation which helped relieve the burden of hard times. Making it successfully was something of a challenge, also, for women who needed to take their minds off their money troubles.

"Whatever its origin, by the 1940s it had become a standard among pieced designs, as basic to the quilter's pattern file as the casserole was to her recipe file. Evidence for this turned up in countless attic trunks during the last five years or so when many people were re-evaluating the quilts left them by the previous generations. The search through old family quilts often revealed at least one Double Wedding Ring.

"In most examples we have seen, the open space in the center of the rings is usually cut in one piece ...Sometimes the pieced rings are appliquéd over this piece, perhaps because this procedure seems easier than inserting it into the rings. However, the pieced version looks better, in our opinion...It isn't the easiest of patterns, but not unreasonably difficult."

Little did Bonnie Leman realize the extent of devotion to the pattern among her readers. In subsequent issues many quilt historians and experts offered their own opinions.

Jonathan Holstein, in a letter printed in the September 1978 issue, built a strong case for the Double Wedding Ring quilt to be of 20th-century origin. "I was interested in the article on the Double Wedding Ring pattern in your June 1978 issue. Though both the Orlofsky and Hinson books say that the pattern is a 19th-century one, we have never seen a quilt using it which in design, materials or workmanship appeared to us to be of a date earlier than the 20th century, and we know of none dated in the body of the quilt, or firmly documented as having been made before the 1920s or 1930s. If anyone actually knows of one which can be firmly dated in some way in the 19th or even early 20th centuries—and is not just thought to have been made then—we would very much like to know about it.

"I think it likely that the design first appeared in the

late 1920s or early '30s in one of those regularly featured magazine or newspaper articles on quilt design. This dating would account for its absence from the Finley book (published in 1927) and presence in the Hall book (published in 1935), as noted in your article. Perhaps an older quilter can remember the first time she saw this pattern used in the Midwest, where it was most popular. If, as the article says, it had 'by the 1940s... become a standard among pieced designs,' that was a situation realized only in the Midwest. It had been a rare pattern in the East until quite recently....As for there not being 'even folk tales about it to satisfy our curiosity,' this would be accounted for by its recent origin.

"And as for its being...in the minds of many people...*the* patchwork quilt, this would again be true only in part of the country. And I do not think it is one of the few that could stand alone as an instantly recognizable symbol of American patchwork. I would think that honor would go to the truly ancient designs—Nine Patch Block, Variable Star, Wild Goose Chase, Star of Bethlehem, Irish Chain, etc.—which have been used in making huge numbers of quilts over the centuries and are known both across this country and in other countries where quilts are made or admired.

"Further, I don't think the Double Wedding Ring pattern became popular during the Depression because it was 'essentially a scrap quilt.' In fact, the centers of this pattern require whole cloth, as was pointed out in the article, and there were in that period hundreds of common block-style designs which used scraps entirely, needing no whole cloth in their making. Such designs were well known to most quilt makers. I think the pattern became popular because of the sentimental appeal to women of the joined rings idea."

Bonnie Leman did not totally agree and replied with an editor's note: "The article in question tried to make the point that the DWR was a scrap quilt *with a difference*. It said, 'although facts about the design elude us, it is likely that it began to be a big favorite in the Depression period of the '20s and '30s because it is essentially a scrap quilt—the only kind most people could afford to make in those lean days—yet it was a scrap quilt with a joyful and romantic connotation which helped relieve the burden of hard times. Making it successfully was something of a challenge, also, for women who needed to take their minds off their money troubles."

Other readers joined the fray and used *Quilter's Newsletter Magazine* as their forum. Alice Bumbardner, a quilter from Pennsylvania, was quoted in the January 1979 issue. "I definitely think the Double Wedding Ring is an old pattern and a classic. My grandmother's ancestors arrived in this country from Germany in 1780. When I was young, grandmother always had a quilt set up in her dining room, and I definitely remember seeing the Double Wedding Ring on her bed. The very last quilting she did was in the early '30s—after that she had to tie them because of failing eyesight—so the DWR was made well before that. Its popularity was not confined to the Midwest, either; it was not a rare pattern in the East. My grandmother lived in a small town east of Pittsburgh. I would like to remind Mr. Holstein that cotton percale could be bought for 10¢ a yard during the Depression, even in 1937. Grandmother always purchased pastels for alternating blocks and backing. Also most of the younger generation don't know a Wild Goose Chase or an Irish Chain from a left-handed monkey wrench, but they sure do know a DWR when they see one. In 1929 Ruth Finley wrote in her *Old Patchwork Quilts*, 'No well known pattern was evolved after 1880...'" The true answer to Mr. Holstein's letter can be found on page 17 of QN #66 (Apr. '75). The fifth paragraph of a reprint of a 1930 clipping written by Carlie Sexton for *Successful Farming Magazine* says, 'The Double Wedding Ring has many names—The Rainbow, Around the World, King Tut are some of the names. It is not a new pattern, however, as some are inclined to think, for one of my readers asked me about the pattern a long time ago and said they had an old quilt of this pattern but could not cut the pattern off. Then, all at once like an epidemic, they were being made all over the country....'"

Edna Paris Ford, a well-known writer about quilts was quoted in the January 1979 issue of *Quilter's Newsletter Magazine*. "Hang in there, Bonnie, and don't back down on your statements concerning the DWR quilt pattern. In *The Great American Cover-Up* there is a DWR dated circa 1870 which was a gift to the museum [The Baltimore Museum of Art] from Dr. William Rush Dunton, Jr. If you look at the picture, you can see why the pattern in this appliqué form was not popular with most quiltmakers. Sewing all those tiny pieces together, then appliquéing them onto a top would be like making two quilt tops. A friend of mine, age 80, says the first DWR she remembers was made by her grandmother about 1906 as an all-pieced quilt. *Ladies Art Catalog*, 1928, has this pattern as No. 512. In 1931 it was advertised and sold by practically every company selling quilt patterns—McKim, Aunt Martha, Brooks, Wheeler, and more. *Woman's World Magazine*, January 1931, shows a picture of this quilt and the copy reads: "This is adapted from a very old pieced patchwork pattern which was frequently found in a bride's linen chest. What we now call appliqué was once called patchwork or laid-on work." Evidently, sometime in the early 1900s this pattern was adapted (as stated in WWM) to the all-pieced pattern as we know it now.

"And the quilt *did* become popular in the Depression days of the 1930s, as you said, I can remember all the ladies piecing their DWR quilts. I don't know why this pattern became so popular, but I think it was because it was such a bright, cheery pattern and could be made of scraps of print which could be saved or traded for; and when finished there was a definite design that showed up over the entire quilt. Not like those hodge-podge blocks that used 10 or 12 different prints and looked like nothing in particular. This DWR quilt is still one of the most popular and best known patterns in Kentucky and some of the other southern states, and surely we can't be called the 'Midwest.'

"I'm sure, if I had the time, I could go through more old publications, newsprint and books and find other dates as documentation."

Other well-known curators and quilt historians share the belief that the Double Wedding Ring quilt pattern is an early development. Barbara Brackman in *An Encyclopedia of Pieced Quilt Patterns* published in 1984 by Prairie Flower Publishing, Lawrence, Kansas, lists two 19th-century quilts of this design. The first owned by the Shelburne Museum, Shelburne, Vermont, is dated 1825–1850 by that institution. The other, in the collection of The Baltimore Museum of Art, Baltimore, Maryland, is catalogued c. 1870, and illustrated by Dena S. Katzenberg in her book, *The Great American Cover-Up: Counterpanes of the Eighteenth and Nineteenth Centuries*, published by The Baltimore Museum of Art in 1971. Dena Katzenberg, who serves as Consultant Curator of Textiles at the museum, states: "Our Double Wedding Ring quilt came to The Baltimore Museum of Art in 1946 with the Dunton bequest which also included the nucleus Baltimore Album Quilt collection. Dr. William Rush Dunton, an extremely knowledgeable collector who wrote and published his famed *Old Quilts*, assembled his artifacts early in the 20th century. He owned many fine old quilts of mid-19th century.

"Reference our Double Wedding Ring—although the fabrics are all of faded solid colors, they do include colors post the aniline processes. The quilt's muslin surfaces and handwork stitches lead me to believe a dating of third quarter 19th century an accurate one.

"You may wish to note the Kretsinger-Hall book, published 1935, plate LVIII, page 193. This photograph has a remark by the author at the bottom stating it's 'a very fine example of this popular old pattern.'"

Karey Bresenhan included what she and her co-author Nancy O'Bryant Puentes considered to be a 19th-century example in their 1986 book, *Lone Stars: A Legacy of Texas Quilts: 1936–1956*. In the caption that accompanies the illustration, the authors state why they felt this piece was made in the 19th century.

"This graphic Double Wedding has an impact in a photograph or when displayed as a wall hanging that would probably surprise the quiltmaker. The interlocking circles of the rings contain red and white with an indigo set and indigo accents. The background fabric has changed color, possibly because it was home-dyed green, which is fading unevenly to khaki, complicated by some fading of the indigo. It originally was an even more vivid quilt.

"It is hand-pieced and hand-quilted in a double rainbow quilting pattern with large stitches typical of a country quilt made rapidly for cover. Country women frequently had two classifications for their quilts: family quilts for everyday use and company quilts to be put on the guest bed only for visitors. This was obviously in the first category and shows evidence of quick and thrifty construction and extensive hard use. Its borders ripple and the quilt is uneven in width. The indigoes are pieced, probably because the quiltmaker ran out of her chosen fabric and had to make do with another. Hand-carded cotton was used for the batting, and cotton seeds can be felt and also seen if the quilt is held to the light.

"The Double Wedding Ring is often thought of as a twentieth-century quilt pattern and we are accustomed to seeing it in its more usual form employing pastel hues and small percales beloved by brides-to-be quilting in the 1930s. Depression-era quilts also often use much smaller pieces in the rings. This quilt, however, illustrates that the bold piecing and striking solid color choices of a nineteenth-century quiltmaker can result in a very modern look…"

Perhaps the definitive answer regarding the earliest use of the design on American quilts will never be established. Clearly, the motif of interlocking rings is a very old one and can actually be traced far back in history.

In the exhibition, "Glass of the Caesars," presented at The Corning Museum of Glass, Corning, New York, in 1987, a cage cup known as the Cologne Cage Cup, believed to have been made during the fourth century A.D., includes the motif (fig. 2). It is just one of several examples of glass vessels or lamps of the Roman period that have as their basic design feature a cage-like network of circular overlay glass mesh. Jane Shadel Spillman, Curator of Glass at the Corning Museum, recently indicated in a letter: "You might be interested to know that the same pattern occurs on a smaller hanging lamp, which we have just acquired, and on

2. This cage cup was one of 150 ancient Roman objects in the special exhibition, "Glass of the Caesars," that was on view at The Corning Museum of Glass, Corning, N.Y., from April 25 through October 18, 1987. Found in Cologne, the cup is made of colorless glass and translucent red, yellow, and green glass. It was cast and wheel-cut during the fourth century A.D. from a single block of glass. Photograph by Mario Carrieri, courtesy of Olivetti, Milan. (Collection of the Römisch-Germanisches Museum, Cologne, West Germany)

several drinking cups of the same period found in Germany and Italy. The question is whether these were made in the Rhine area or in the Mediterranean."

Another early source for the Double Wedding Ring design might have been the gimmal ring, figure 3, which is a betrothal ring that is composed of two, three, or even more interlocking loops that can be assembled to form a single ring. Those of more complex design were considered puzzles; sometimes they were purposely designed to be difficult to reassemble when taken apart. The most popular form of the gimmal ring consisted of only two separate loops that could be totally separated. During the engagement period one loop was worn by the man; the other by the woman. At the time of the marriage the two rings were fitted together to become the wedding ring for the woman.

The bezel of the gimmal ring was divided so that when the parts were assembled they formed a single ornament. Often the bezel was decorated with a "fede"

or clasped-hands motif. A heart-shaped ornament was also popular. A more elaborate gimmal ring had three loops; the two outer loops were decorated with hands that would interlock when the ring was assembled and the third or middle loop had a heart that was held by the hands. An inscription frequently ran along the facing halves of the hoops. It would be visible only when the hoops were separated. One of the most popular inscriptions from the Renaissance "Quod Deus Coniunxit Homo Non Separet" translates "What God hath joined let no man put asunder."

Gimmal rings were popular throughout much of Europe during the 15th and 16th centuries. It is certain that they were fashioned and used much earlier in both ancient Greece and Rome. Several examples were discovered during the 18th- and early 19th-century excavations of Pompeii.

The gimmal ring probably first reached America when large numbers of Germanic peoples settled in Pennsylvania during the late 17th and early 18th centuries. For the most part, German colonists came to the New World in search of rich farmlands where they quickly established agrarian communities. By nature, the German settler was conservative. Old World customs and social traditions survived for many generations.

3. Gimmal ring. 16th century. Germany. Gold and enamel with high quatrefoil bezel set with a ruby and a diamond. The German inscription reads: "What God has joined together let no man put asunder." It is possible that the idea for a Double Wedding Ring quilt was derived from the European gimmal ring, which is known to have been brought from the Old World to the New by immigrants in the 18th century. Several American gimmal rings of a slightly less complex design are known. The Double Wedding Ring quilt was especially popular in parts of the United States that had a substantial population of Germanic origin. (Zucker Family Collection)

4. Ceramic tile made by J. & J. G. Low, Boston, Massachusetts. Late 19th century. 6″ x 6″. During the 19th century several manufacturers produced objects that incorporated a design similar to the Double Wedding Ring motif. The Low firm was considered one of the most prestigious ceramic firms in America in the late Victorian period.

Decorative motifs similar to the Double Wedding Ring design are known in 19th-century America. Overshot coverlets woven in the home by women during the Colonial period and by professional itinerant male weavers in the 19th century were generally based upon the square or rectangle. Some of the more ambitious weavers' efforts included the wheel or circular motif as well. The coverlet designs might have formed the basis for patterns that became popular with quiltmakers. The Double Chariot Wheel, the Whig Rose, and the Double Wedding Ring quilt might all have evolved from early coverlet designs. The candlewick spread illustrated in figure 1 is another example where the motif might have been borrowed from a coverlet.

By the mid-Victorian period the design appeared on many commercially manufactured products. China makers in the 1860s used it as a decorative motif on dinnerware, and the J. & J. G. Low Art Tile Works of Chelsea, Massachusetts, offered glazed tiles featuring the motif, figure 4, a few decades later.

As indicated earlier in various articles published in *Quilter's Newsletter Magazine*, it seems almost certain that the Double Wedding Ring quilt pattern was popular during the latter part of the 19th century and in the early 20th century, when it was referred to as The Rainbow. A detailed search of old newspapers, sewing magazines, and brochures printed in 1928 by fabric and pattern suppliers has led to the discovery of several illustrated articles and pattern offerings where the Double Wedding Ring pattern is identified. The October 20, 1928 issue of *Capper's Weekly* published in Topeka, Kansas, included an illustration of the quilt pattern and credits Mrs. J. D. Patterson of Wellington, Kansas, for the design. For 15¢ it was possible to order a full-size cutting pattern from the Quilt Block Service, *Capper's Weekly.* It was suggested that by purchasing the pattern the quilter could save "much time and bother, for the pattern gives the actual size of each piece and shows how they are set together." The article indicates that the pattern is also known as The Endless Chain and The Rainbow: "When some good but unknown man conceived the idea of a double wedding ring ceremony it gave his wife an equally good idea. She worked the two circles into a double wedding ring quilt."

Just eleven days later, in the October 31, 1928 issue of the *Kansas City Star*, a fully illustrated detailed pattern was offered under "The Wedding Ring Pattern Makes a Beautiful Quilt" headline. The design is credited to the McKim Studios of Independence, Missouri. The accompanying text suggests that the pattern is already in demand: "The real quilt enthusiasts will delight in the wedding ring pattern, but it is hardly a design for the novice to tackle. Several requests for this quilt pattern have been received, so the painstaking care which this attractive quilt requires seems to be no intimidation. One lady who has made this quilt boasts 720 small blocks in her counterpane—and almost all of these are different. That is the unique idea in this pattern—no two of the wedge-shaped blocks should be alike, or in close proximity if these are alike, at least. It is called the wedding ring design because when the melon-shaped blocks are set together, forming four patches where they join, these make large, perfect circles, overlapping regularly into a really lovely design of linked rings."

The pattern was repeated in the September 28, 1929 issue of the *Kansas City Star*, where the headline reads: "A Favorite Block Returns by Request." The column also indicates that the pattern was copyrighted by the paper in the same year. Evidence implies that when the pattern came to be identified in the period 1928–1930, its popularity spread like prairie wildfire. In the regular feature called "In Our Homes," edited by Mary M. Redford for *The Missouri Ruralist*, she reported on September 15, 1929: "The modern woman has turned to the fad of making old-fashioned quilts. The wedding ring seems to be the most popular design judging from the number of wedding ring quilts which were shown this year."

As the pattern proliferated, various new names were given to it. Numerous variations were also conceived by inventive needlewomen in several parts of the country. Listed below are the most popular names used for the pattern and its variations through the years.

WEDDING RING TYPES

Around the World	Lover's Knot
Baby Bunting	Mohawk Trail
Bay Leaf	Ohio Beauty
Black Beauty	Patriot's Pride
Cathedral Window	Pickle Dish
Circle Upon Circle	Pine Burr
Coiled Rattlesnake	Quilted Rattlesnake
Compass	Rainbow Wedding Ring
Double Wedding Bands	The Rainbow
Double Wedding Ring	Rings Around the World
The Endless Chain	Snake Trail
Four Leaf Clover	Spider Web
Friendship Knot	The Star Chain
Golden Wedding Ring	Sweetwater Quilt
Here Comes the Bride	Tea Leaf
Indian Wedding Ring	Wedding Ring Chain
King Tut	When Circles Get Together
Ladies Beautiful Star	Whispering Leaves
Lafayette Orange Peel	Wonder of the World

During the early 1930s, a series of myths developed about the Double Wedding Ring quilt. In a brochure, *Patchwork Quilts in History*, signed by Grandmother Clark and issued in 1932 by W.L.M. Clark, Inc., of St. Louis, Missouri, the origin of the pattern is related to the War Between the States (fig. 5).

 **Patchwork Quilts in History**

Fifty Years Ago—Double Wedding Ring

 In the decade following the Civil War quilt making was very popular. The economic condition found men as well as women making quilts. Grandma was making her share as usual and had quite a number to her credit. Among her collection was one she particularly favored and was saving for her favorite niece's wedding whenever that may be. Jane's fiance who had been wounded in the Battle of Antietam, in 1862, spent many years in the hospital, but finally returned home and the wedding was planned. "Grandma," said Jane, "we will not be able to have our rings until later." Grandma, however, solved the problem. "My child, I'll furnish the rings. You shall have my favorite quilt and we will call it the Double Wedding Ring."

"In the decade following the Civil War quilt making was very popular. The economic condition found men as well as women making quilts. Grandma was making her share as usual and had quite a number to her credit. Among her collection was one she particularly favored and was saving for her favorite niece's wedding whenever that may be. Jane's fiancé who had been wounded in the Battle of Antietam, in 1862, spent many years in the hospital, but finally returned home and the wedding was planned. 'Grandma,' said Jane, 'we will not be able to have our rings until later.' Grandma, however, solved the problem. 'My child, I'll furnish the rings. You shall have my favorite quilt and we will call it the Double Wedding Ring.'"

Cuesta Benberry explained in a letter to me that one of the ways the pattern reached an ever-widening audience in the 1930s was through the newspaper column "Nancy Page Quilt Club." The premise is that

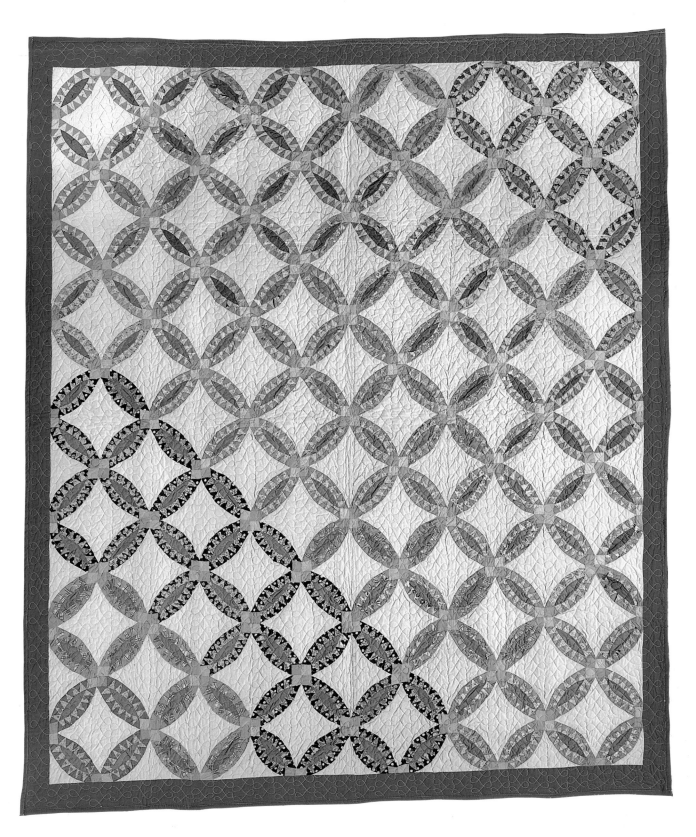

6. Indian Wedding Ring or Pickle Dish. c. 1935. 84″ x 72″. Both solid pastel fabrics and printed fabrics were used by the maker to create this splendid bedcover. Greens, mauves, pinks, and purples predominate. Central patches are pink and yellow. The central panel is surrounded by a vibrant blue border, and the same blue is used as the backing of the quilt. The quilting was executed in a wave pattern on a foot-treadle sewing machine.

Nancy Page was the leader/teacher who worked with a mythical group. There's usually "conversation" at the beginning of the column. Nancy may bring a "new" pattern to the group, or one of the "members" may bring a pattern (new to her), as she asks Nancy questions about the pattern. Nancy often gives "historical data about a new pattern." The Nancy Page column was written by Florence La Gauke. One of her extensive illustrated features from the early 1930s (though undated) proved to be rich in historical detail

7. Sampler quilt. 1935–1945. 84¼" x 72". The center of this unique bedcover is a Double Wedding Ring design that is surrounded by traditional quilt blocks appliquéd onto a blue-green background. A red-orange border surrounds the central panel of the quilt, making a handsome contrast to the background color. The quilting is done in an overall waffle pattern, with a variety of quilting designs used in the individual blocks. The two Double Wedding Ring motifs have floral quilting.

and crammed with practical hints for the contemporary quilter: "Nancy was at a loss to understand the popularity of the Double Wedding Ring pattern. She wondered whether folks were thinking in terms of divorces or in terms of the double wedding ring ceremony. She thought possibly they believed the double ring ceremony might prove more binding in these days of easy change.

"It is quite true that she saw another reason for the popularity of this pattern. It called for small blocks which used up the many, many scraps left over from the popular print dresses. And putting together the small blocks could be used for pick-up work. All the rings could be pieced before the quilt was put together... it is wise, of course, to keep all the colors in about the same key or depth or intensity, otherwise a color rises and hits you in the face as you look at the quilt...

"This quilt, like all well-made quilts, needs careful sewing and frequent pressing. Lay the pieced blocks on a flat table frequently to be sure that you are not drawing them out of shape."

Nancy cautioned her readers lest they grow careless in piecing their quilt. A bedcover is beautiful only when it lies flat and smooth. She also had specific ideas about quilting designs.

"Small diamond quilting is suggested for the four-square block and for the inner part.

"Parallel lines of quilting running around the ring and broken only where the rings cross with the four patch make a good quilting.

"The edges of this quilt may be scalloped to correspond with rings or the edges may be straight. In either case it is wise to bind the edges after the quilting is done and quilt has been removed from the frame..."

While many were writing about the Double Wedding Ring design and publishing illustrations and offering paper patterns, the McKim Studios offered in their 1931 catalogue, *Designs Worth Doing*, a kit for the Rainbow Wedding Ring.

"This is the Double Wedding Ring pattern that is so justly popular once again, only it is worked out in blending tints of peach, pink, orchid, blue, green and yellow, each rainbow ending with an orange or ivory square; background white. Should you want this in a very large size for a spread with a lovely scalloped edge, which requires 13½ yards of material, our quilt number 304M at $5.00 is planned to finish 90 to 94 inches square, depending on your seams. Number 304T at $4.00 is regulation or large twin size finishing about 75 by 92 inches. Either includes all materials cut for entire top.

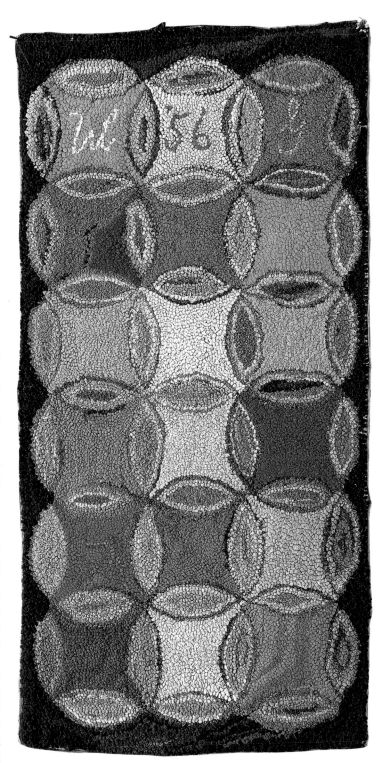

8. Hooked rug. Dated " '56" (probably indicating 1956), and initiated "WG." Figure 1 illustrates a late 19th-century candlewick spread in the Double Wedding Ring design, and here is a colorful small rug of recent years testifying to the effectiveness of the Double Wedding Ring design in another medium.

"Cutting out a quilt is a rather long and tedious process by hand, and accuracy is so important. We have made it possible to get some of the most beautiful quilt patterns ready-cut, and among these none is more lovely than the Wedding Ring in rainbow tints. Materials are fine, fast color tints, and either 304M or 304T will make the ample size which is so desirable in these days when patchwork makes the favorite top cover.

"Special quilting designs perforated on heavy paper to stamp many times may be ordered as No. 296 at 25¢. This is a spider-web for the large pillow-shaped white block and flower with leaves to fit the ellipse-shaped block. A box of stamping wax is number 206 at 25¢. Pattern alone is in our patchwork pattern book 631A at 15¢. This book also contains eleven other quilt patterns."

While most of the Double Wedding Ring quilts in this book were pieced and quilted by hand it is evident that some were fashioned with the aid of a sewing machine. The remarkable Indian Wedding Ring quilt in figure 6 appears to have been hand-stitched, but a close look at the back reveals that the quilting was accomplished on a foot-powered treadle machine. This was quite a feat,

for the quilting design required much skill on the part of the maker.

The Double Wedding Ring pattern remained popular, and in the 1940s, at the Wayne County, Ohio, Annual Fair, a new exhibition category was established for three quilt designs: Double Wedding Ring, Grandmother's Flower Garden, and Dresden Plate. In 1949, premium prizes were offered for each of these patterns. All other quilts, regardless of pattern, were exhibited in a fourth category.

Even today the Double Wedding Ring and several variations are the most popular exhibits at traditional quilt shows such as the annual Kutztown Folk Festival held at Kutztown, Pennsylvania.

Obviously, the Double Wedding Ring pattern will be eternally popular. I have had tremendous fun putting together this collection of quilts in this one design, for I found something fascinating in each one, and I very much hope that you will find them to be equally interesting both singly and as a group. Also, by using the patterns and instructions created by Carter Houck that are included at the back of this book, it will be possible for you to create a Double Wedding Ring quilt that will be cherished by future generations.

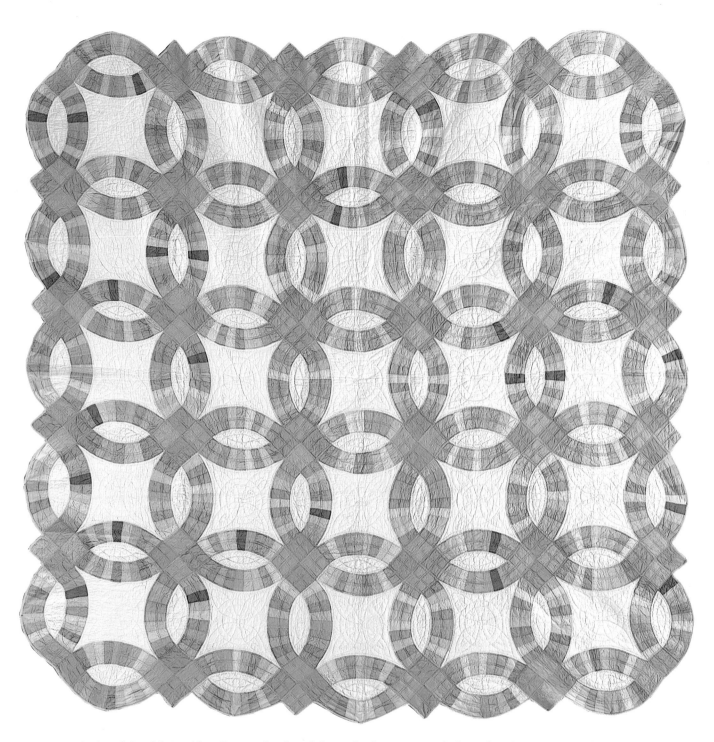

9. Amish Double Wedding Ring quilt. The solid pastel colors are typical of Amish and Mennonite quilts of the period. Most Amish quilts were made with black or dark backgrounds and tend to be more somber than this example. The quilting on this piece is very well done. As Ruth Stewart, an old-time quilter, observed: "If you make the stitches too long and get your toes caught in them of a night, then hit'll be you to blame."[1] Indiana; 1945–1955; 83″ x 80½″.

10. The edges of this patriotic Double Wedding Ring are scalloped and trimmed with small red, white, and blue triangles. The back is white cotton. Virginia Snow, an author of the 1930s, sought to promote the use of domestic products, thus helping the American economy. "Just a word now about the threads and Berkshire and Becket silks best suited for the fine work, and best of all they represent American labor with exclusively American capital.... You have the opportunity; now is the time for every woman in a simple way to satisfy her needs, to help America in her hour of need."[2] 1930–1940; 79″ x 71″.

11. Made by an Afro-American artist in Georgia, this dramatically colorful piece is the quilt that inspired the formation of the collection. The quilt appears to be filled with unprocessed cotton balls. Some quiltmakers preferred to use wool, for it made their bedcovers especially warm. Atlanta, Georgia; 1930–1940; 86″ x 73¼″.

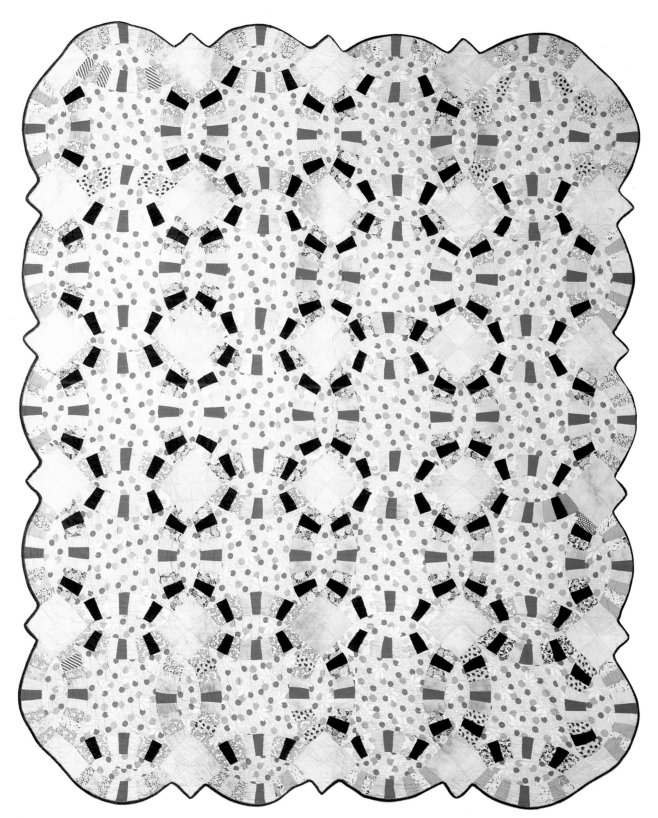

12. The color values of the Art Deco-style fabrics in this quilt might well have been altered by repeated washings. One quiltmaker described her efforts to launder quilts: "Well, it wasn't no easy job. We'd take and put them in a big tub of water and put in plenty of home-made soap and rub 'n' rub. Then we'd lay them out on a bench an' padde 'em. Had a paddlin' stick, they called it, and just come down with all the power in both hands, and everywhere you struck that quilt, you'd make a clean place."[3] Midwest; 1930–1940; 82″ x 76″.

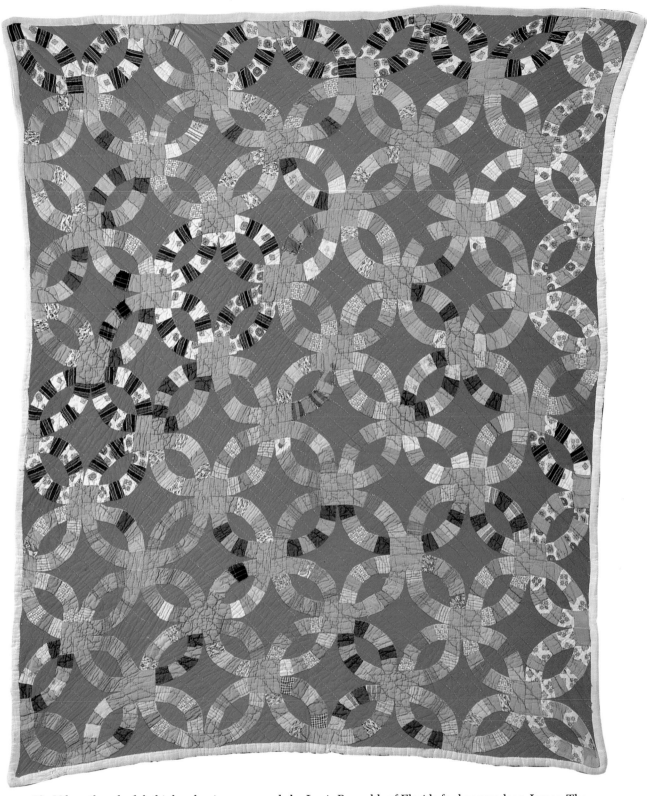

13. Vibrantly colorful, this lovely piece was made by Jessie Reynolds of Florida for her grandson, James. The needlework is not elegant, but the design and color are wonderfully alive. Delray Beach, Florida; c. 1935; 69″ x 56½″.

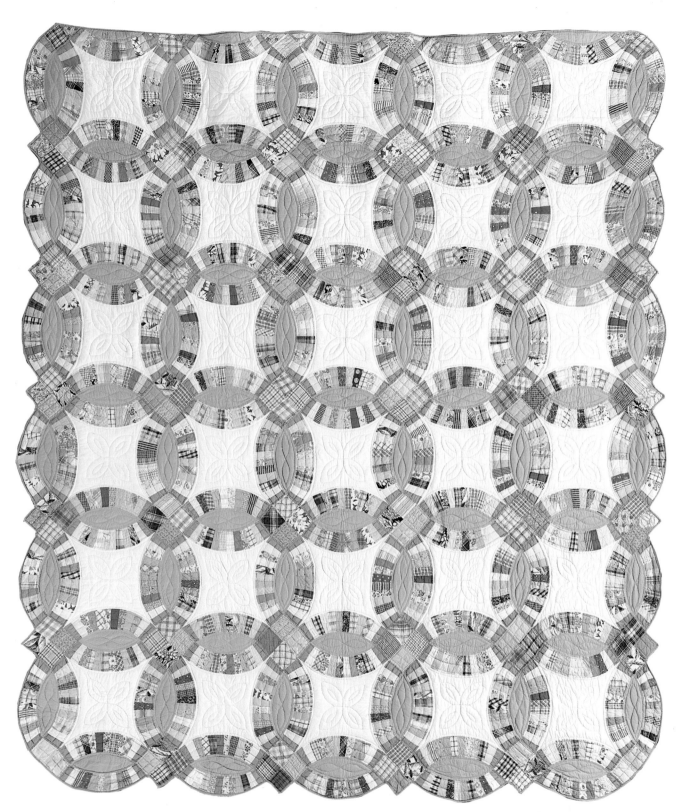

14. The skillful maker of this quilt thought carefully about her composition. A scalloped edge is used on three sides; the straight edge at the top provided a comfortable way of covering the pillows at the head of the bed. By using pale green as a frame for the intersecting blocks, the quiltmaker unified the quilt with the color combination of green and lavender. 1935–1940; 88½″ x 76″.

15. It seems that this quilt was probably intended as a summer spread, for there is almost no batting. The center panels are quilted with sunflowers. The lozenges are quilted with a four-square center design, extended by lozenges. The legs of the circles are quilted all over, and the connecting blocks between the legs have waffle quilting. Albany, New York; 1930–1940; 90″ x 76″.

16. The central panels of the Double Wedding Ring design are waffle quilted. The lozenges are outlined in parallel lines. The border is quilted in a running stitch that extends from the top to the bottom of the quilt. It is evident that the artist lavished great pains on this quilt, for careful attention has been paid to color balance and overall visual impact. Monterey, California; c. 1935; 86″ x 66″.

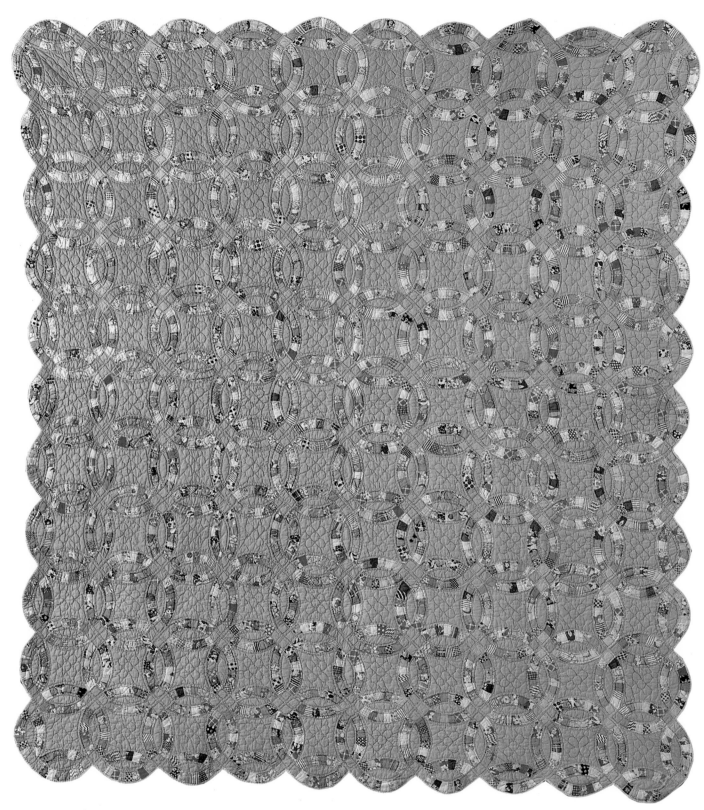

17. In Wedding Ring quilts made in the South, one often finds the additional embellishment of embroidered floral motifs on the four patches intersecting the circle design. On a quilt where the piecework is very small, such as this example, it was simply not practical to include this refinement. Missouri; 1930–1940; 74½″ x 72½″.

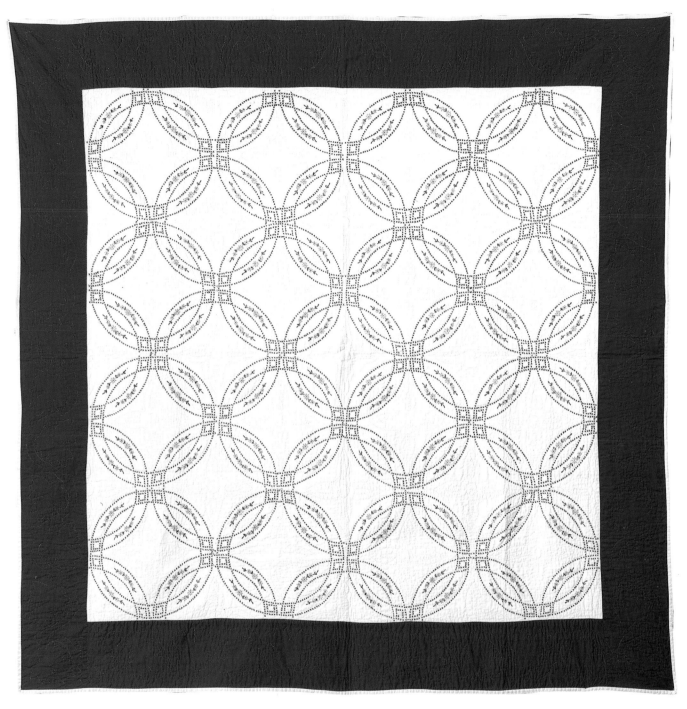

18. In this unusual piece the legs of the rings are executed in blue cross-stitch with a yellow and green cross-stitch floral pattern. The four-square intersection is also embroidered in blue. The blue outer border is quilted with an unusual maple-leaf and running-vine motif. Similar examples were published in popular magazines during the 1930s and 1940s. New England; c. 1935; 77″ x 77″.

19. This variation of the Double Wedding Ring design is called Indian Wedding Ring or Pickle Dish. Here is a very handsome rendition of the design—coolly colorful and precisionist in the way that the blue and white triangles provide a crisp contrast to the stripes of the melon patches and the Spiderweb quilting. 1935–1945; 81″ x 71″.

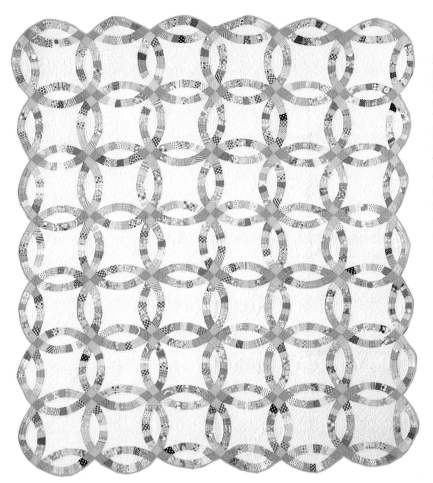

20. This quilt is especially delicate because of the narrowness of the legs of the rings. Ruby S. McKim, in *One Hundred and One Patchwork Patterns* (1962), advised: "This Double Wedding Ring quilt should not be attempted by anyone except a real quilt enthusiast. The friend from whom we got this pattern boasts 720 small blocks in her counterpane, nearly all different." She had specific ideas about quilting patterns as well. "A Spiderweb design is recommended for the large pillow-shaped white block and flower with leaves to fit the ellipse-shaped block." 1935–1945; 81″ x 71″.

21. This quilt literally dances with color, for the legs of the rings are constructed of small, solid, bright pieces. The junctions of the rings are elongated squares of various colors. The background is champagne. The quilt is bound and backed with pink polished cotton. The center panels of the rings are quilted with two concentric circles framed by feathers. The lozenges are quilted with a circle embellished with elongated ovals on two sides. 1940–1950; 87″ x 87″.

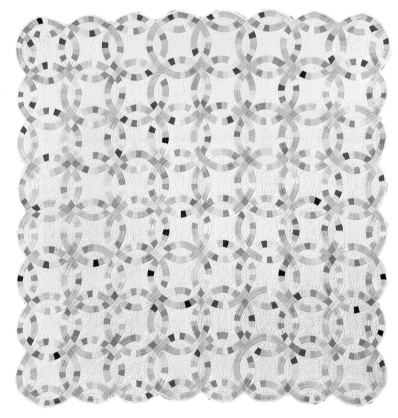

22. How very handsomely the colors of the fall season are mirrored in this fine piece! The yellow and olive-brown patches at the intersections set the overall tone, and the bright prints in the rings flicker like autumn leaves. Pennsylvania; 1935–1945; 84″ x 74″.

23. During the Depression financial conditions frequently made cloth enough of a luxury to encourage conservation. No scrap was too small to be saved. This may partially account for the popularity of patterns, such as Snake Trail and Double Wedding Ring, which consumed many small scraps. If a particular color was especially difficult to obtain, it became a prized possession in quiltmaking circles, where the most-cherished materials were shared only with close friends. Southern U.S.; 1930–1940; 87″ x 82″.

24. An unusual feature of this quilt is the two quite different shades of red used in the rings and the inner border. Elaborate floral designs are quilted into the center patches of the ring motifs. Midwest; 1935–1945; 94″ x 71″.

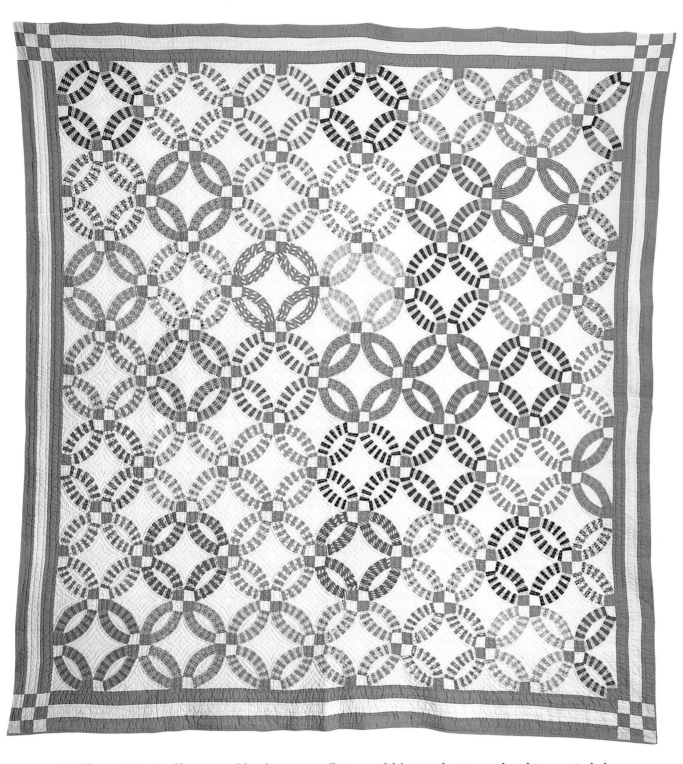

25. The precisionist effect created by the very small pieces of fabric in the rings makes this a particularly interesting Double Wedding Ring. 1930–1940; 93″ x 87″.

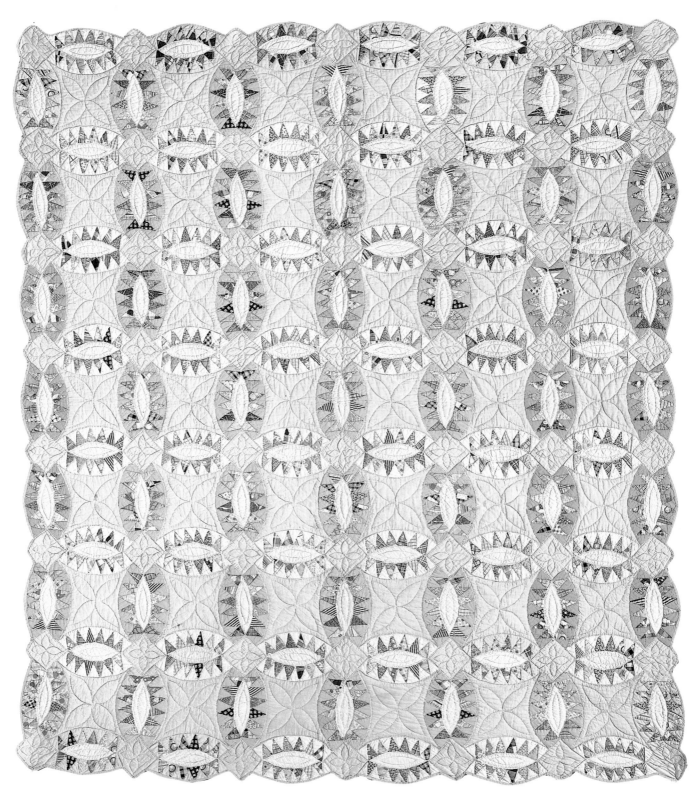

26. It is the soft palette of pink and yellow in this Pickle Dish design that makes this lovely piece so immediately appealing. The Pickle Dish design is nearly identical to a pattern called Pine Burr, which was especially popular in the South. 1930–1940; 83″ x 74″.

27. Quilter Rose Brite of Warren City, Kentucky, said of old-fashioned quilting bees: "We sewed with a red-hot needle and a burning thread!"[4] Her friend, Thala Thompson, particularly enjoyed quilting the Double Wedding Ring pattern, as the solid-color areas were large enough to exhibit her skills. Everyday household objects were useful for making the quilting patterns—a thimble could be used to make small circles; a glass, larger ones. 1930–1940; 85″ x 82¼″.

28. In this Golden Wedding Ring quilt the typical Double Wedding Ring design has been enhanced by the inclusion of broken, six-point stars in the center panels. The pattern for this design was offered for sale in the October 1934 issue of *The Royal Neighbor*. The advertisement states: "To attain the Happy Golden Wedding Day is one of the most important events in all lives. This new quilt pattern is dedicated to those who can look back over 50 years of happy married life." The patterns were available through the R.N.A. Art Department, 707 Locust Street, Des Moines, Iowa. Eldon, Missouri; c. 1930; 81¼″ x 73″.

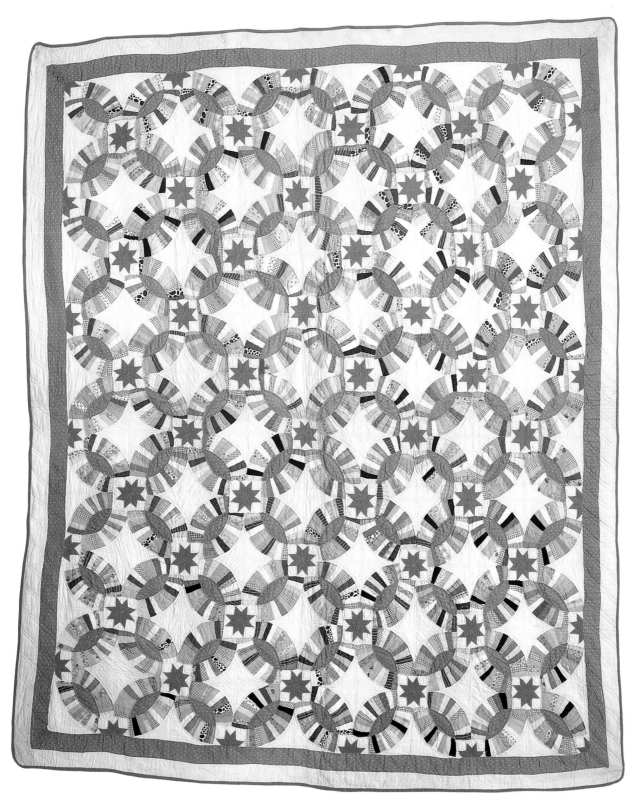

29. Once owned by Bernice Johnson of Franklin, Johnson County, Indiana, this quilt has the unusual embellishment of bright red stars that punctuate the intersections of the rings. It is a happy quilt for a happy occasion, for attached to the back of the quilt is a handwritten note stating: "Grandmother Wyatt made it for my wedding gift. 1928." Indiana; 1928; 82″ x 74″.

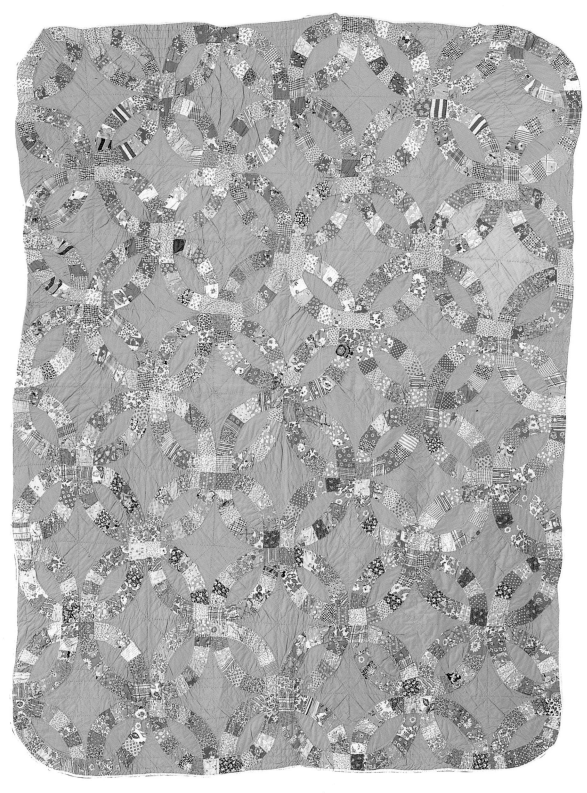

30. In spite of its having been crudely executed, this piece is still perky and very appealing. Texas; c. 1950; 74″ x 68″.

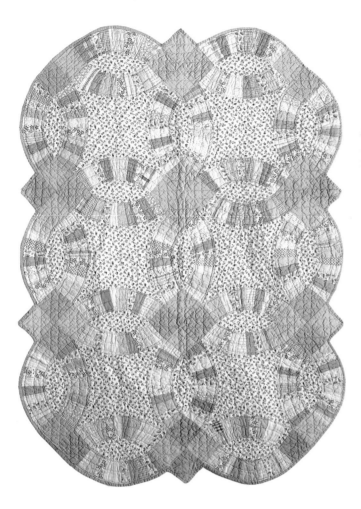

31. The sprigged cotton makes an appropriate background for the pastel colors of the rings in this crib quilt. 1935–1940; 43″ x 31″.

32. It is the soft yet bright colors and the fine quilting that speak to us here. It is not too often that one finds a good crib quilt in the Double Wedding Ring design, probably because it is a difficult pattern to execute well in a diminutive size. Houston, Texas; 1935–1945; 57″ x 37½″.

33. The predominantly black background and the pastel rings of this rustic piece might well be found on many Amish and Mennonite textiles. It is obvious that the maker of this bedcover did not have enough corduroy to finish the task and was forced to include crushed velvets of strikingly different textures and hues. The quilting is minimal. Dolphia Elins of New Loyston, Tennessee, recently recalled: "Back when I was first married we just used anything we could get to make quilts out of. Take men's clothes and cut the best out of them you know.... They's awful thick where they was made out of thick material. They'd tack them, and just called 'em comforts. They's heavy too. But them old heavy wool quilts felt good then, on a cold night."[5] 1940–1950; 67½″ x 48½″.

34. This charming version of the Double Wedding Ring design is one of the most interesting in the collection. The predominant colors of the printed fabrics are pink, yellow, blue, gray, orange, green, and red—all being versions or "colorways" of the same design. The quilting is also most attractively done. 1945–1955; 86½″ x 69″.

35. How elegantly the bright red melons and intersection blocks contribute to the unified composition of this quilt, and the narrow red binding adds just the right touch to the whole. 1930–1950; 78″ x 70″.

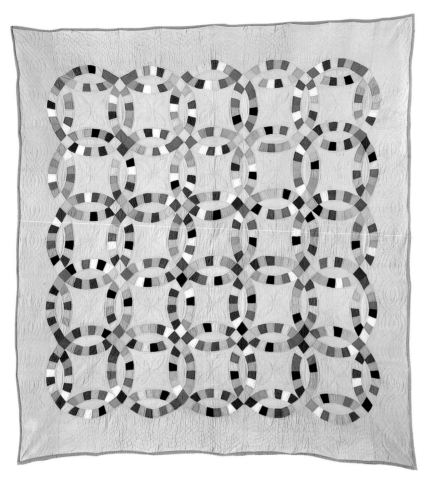

36. Most Amish women probably passed patterns between themselves. They seldom ordered kits or paper patterns from professional quilt studios, which flourished throughout the 1920s, 1930s, and 1940s. The Amish needleworker, who made this quilt, was probably not even aware of firms like the Needlecraft Supply Company of 800 North Clark Street, Chicago, Illinois, which in 1938 supplied kits for Double Wedding Ring quilts, ready-cut in rainbow tints. The Needlecraft prepackaged project featured squares in pumpkin and ivory, with blending pastels ranging from honeydew, pink, and orchid to sky, green, and yellow. Also included were two special quilting patterns, perforated to stamp onto all-white background blocks. Goshen, Indiana; 1930–1940; 82″ x 75″.

37. Here is a wonderful example of how a brilliant stained-glass effect can be achieved with fabric. It was was made in 1950 by Esther Enger, an Amish quiltmaker of Holmes County, Ohio. The quilt is one of a pair; the other piece is illustrated in figure 43. The center panels are quilted with the popular Amish Spiderweb design, and the outline of a spider has been added to some of the webs. Ohio; dated 1950 in the quilting; 92″ x 73″.

38. Only a glance is necessary to tell us how beautifully this quilt has been made—not only in the expert selection of color but also in the high quality of the quilted designs that contribute so much to its beauty. Note the three patches of solid black. New England; 1930–1940; 86½ x 78″.

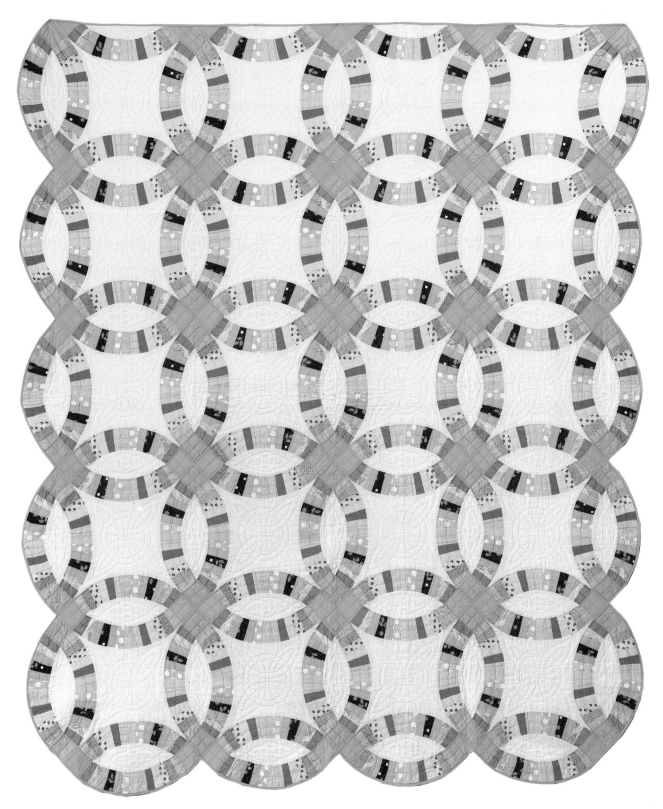

39. A quilt should give delight as well as warmth—and what particularly delights us in this piece? It is the blue-and-white polka-dot patches that dance around the surface of the quilt like miniature balloons to bolster our spirits. 1930–1940; 86″ x 72¾″.

40 (top) and 41 (bottom). This pair of quilts shows how very effectively the Double Wedding Ring design can be made with just two colors rendered with small patches in well-contrasting colors. Figure 40: 1935–1945; 83″ x 68″. Figure 41: Texas; 1935–1945; 89″ x 76″. This quilt has hearts quilted in the intersection patches.

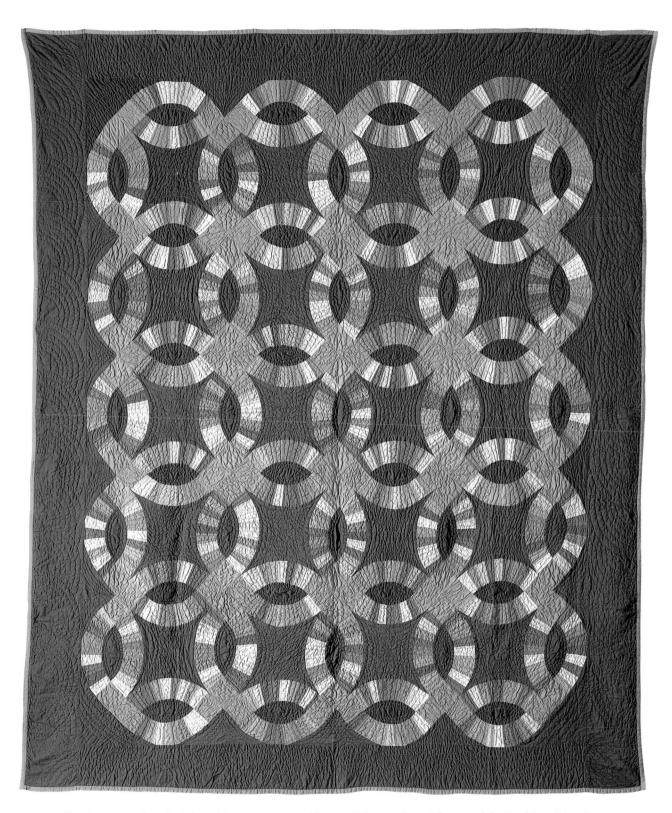

42. Here is another dark Amish beauty enhanced by much fine quilting. The use of the Wedding Ring design by the Amish is curious, for in Amish society jewelry of all sorts, including wedding bands, was not permitted. Amish quiltmakers probably first borrowed this pattern from their "English" neighbors and came to admire it for the many ways that color could be arranged to change the design. Ohio; 1935-1945; 89½″ x 75″.

43. This is the jewel-like companion to the Amish Double Wedding Ring quilt illustrated in figure 37. This piece was made by Anna Weaver, also in 1950, in Holmes County, Ohio. She was the sister of Esther Enger, who made the other quilt. Ohio; dated 1950 in the quilting; 92″ x 77″.

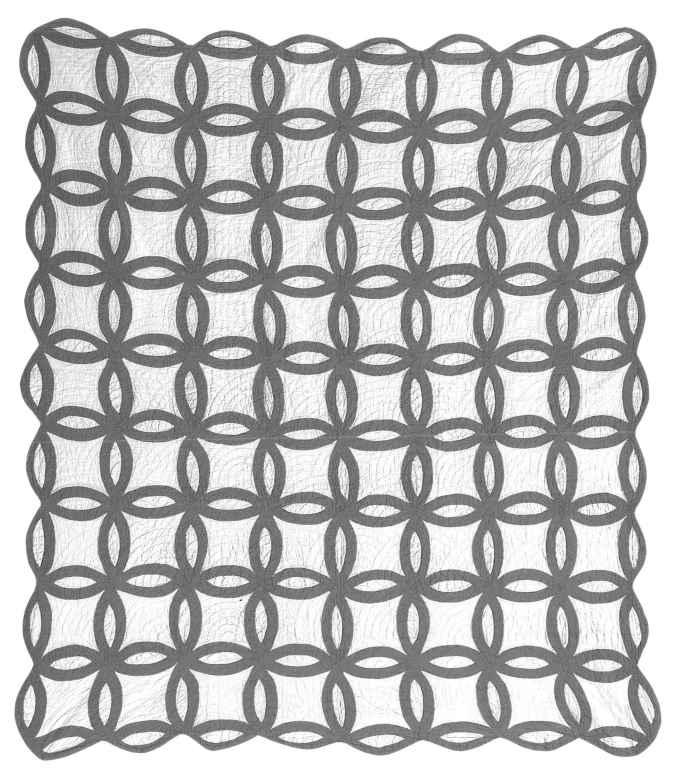

44. Although this quilt is rather crudely made, it still makes a very effective graphic statement. Note that in this piece the rings have been cut from red fabric and appliquéd to the white background. In the late 1930s, the catalogue *Colonial Quilts* was published by the Needlework Department of the *St. Louis Post Dispatch*. The catalogue offered a Double Wedding Ring pattern, and the text states it is "the most popular of any quilt that has come to us through the ages." Pennsylvania; 1930–1940; 78½″ x 70″.

45. This effective piece in just two shades of blue is another example where the Wedding Rings have been appliquéd onto the background. The large panels have an unusual quilting design of Maltese crosses in squares. 1930–1945; 89″ x 72½″.

46. Mary K. Borkowski, who made this quilt, during the 1970s and early 1980s became recognized as an important contemporary quiltmaker. Her pieces were acquired by numerous national museums and were exhibited throughout the world. In this piece, the centers of the rings are embellished with a red button, and a decorative flower-and-vine motif makes a delightful border. In a letter written while she was making this Double Wedding Ring, she said: "I have the small quilt about one-half done. I cannot see well enough anymore to sew all those tiny blocks together, so these are appliquéd on one sheet of pure muslin, in red, white, and blue." Dayton, Ohio; dated 1988; 55″ x 55″.

42

47. What fun this quilt is! It contains a bright and beautiful patch bag of fabrics guaranteed to put a smile on any quiltlover's face. A quiltmaker was recently quoted as saying: "I learnt to quilt from my mother, and she's still quilting. Past 90 and still quilting.... Yeah, I like to quilt. Get up here in this attic room and just set and quilt all by myself. Nobody to bother me. I'd druther quilt than anything I ever done."[6] 1955–1945; 78″ x 64″.

48. In decided contrast to the quilt illustrated in figure 47, which is so bright and breezy, this handsome piece is quite sober and dignified. The quiltmaker has used a wide variety of figured wools and cottons that work well together to make a very satisfying whole. 1935–1945; 81″ x 66½″.

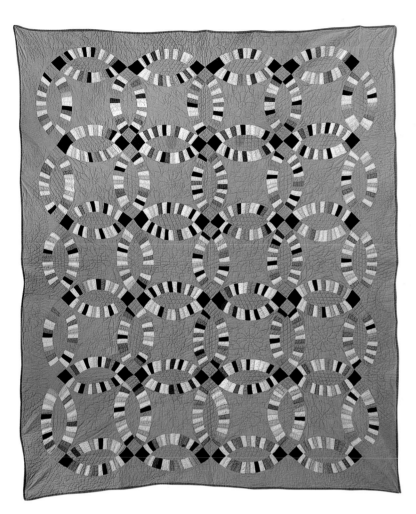

49 (top) and 50 (bottom). Here are two studies in purple. The Amish piece has a rich background covered with patches in intense lights and darks, while the second piece is very subdued in tone, for the purple has a gray cast. Figure 49: Ohio or Indiana; 1935–1945; 87″ x 74½″. Figure 50: 1930–1940; 83½″ x 81½″.

45

51. Here is a fat and sassy quilt! It is obvious that the artist liked her patches to be both bright and well fed—
no skinny Wedding Rings for her! Note the interesting way that she has finished off the corners at top right and
bottom left. Probably Sea Island, Georgia; 1935–1945; 81″ x 64″.

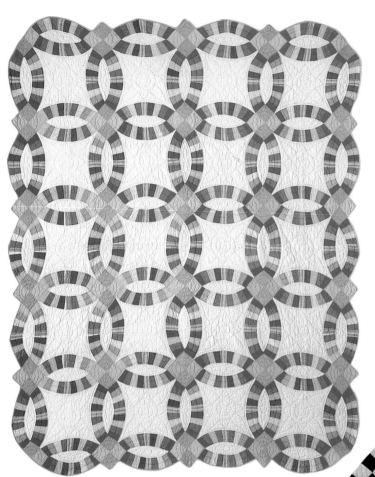

52 (top) and 53 (bottom). These two Double Wedding Rings work well together, for while both are made with almost entirely solid-color fabrics and no prints, the first quilt is rather subdued in its effect, and the second is bright and bold. Note that in the top quilt the maker has placed a patch of red-white-and-blue-striped fabric in the center of each leg. Figure 52: Ohio; 1930–1940; 84″ x 68″. Figure 53: Amish quilt from Holmes County, Ohio; 1930–1945; 81″ x 66½″.

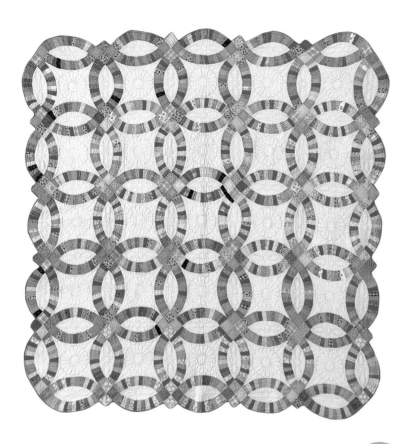

54 (top) and 55 (bottom). Pink is the strong color in both these delightful creations, and they are illustrated together so that one can see what different effects can be achieved with similar color schemes. Lest any doubt the popularity of the Double Wedding Ring design, note the following from the *Missouri Ruralist* for February 1, 1931: "The vogue for quilts has swept the countryside. One fair I attended had a display of them in which there were 161 entries of the Wedding Ring design alone." Figure 54: Maine; 1930–1945; 69″ x 70″. Figure 55: c. 1940; 82″ x 72″.

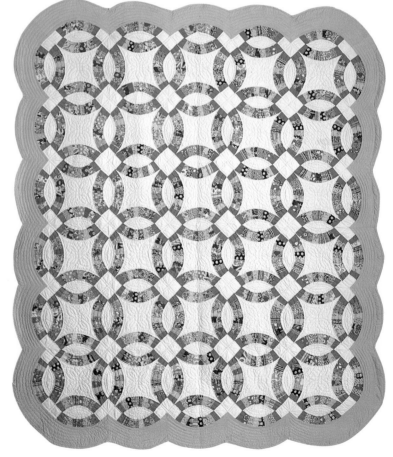

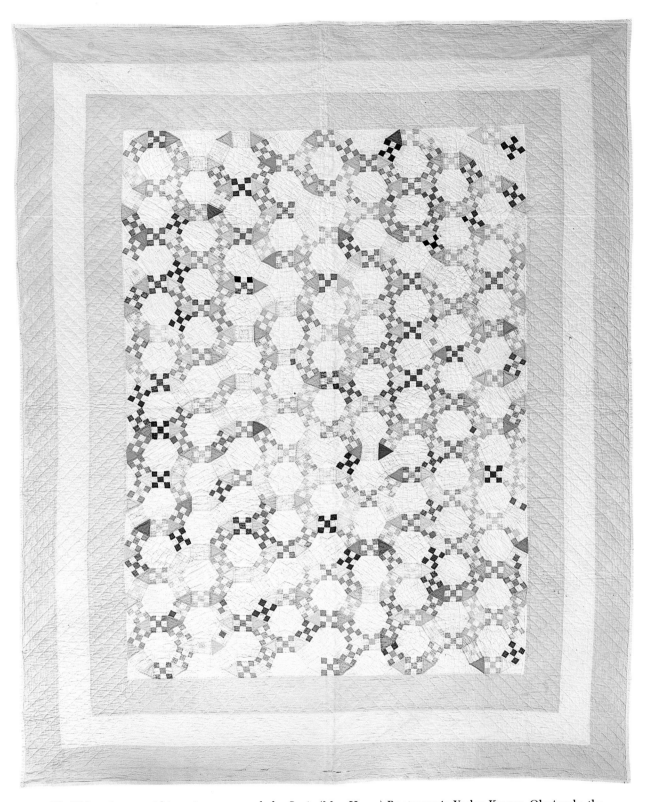

56. This quite astonishing piece was made by Susie (Mrs. Harry) Bontrager in Yoder, Kansas. Obviously, the artist had a special feeling for Nine Patch blocks, for she has used them in bright colors to make her rings in conjunction with triangle patches. The happy result is a wonderfully pleasing variation on the Double Wedding Ring pattern. Kansas; c. 1935; 95½″ x 78½″.

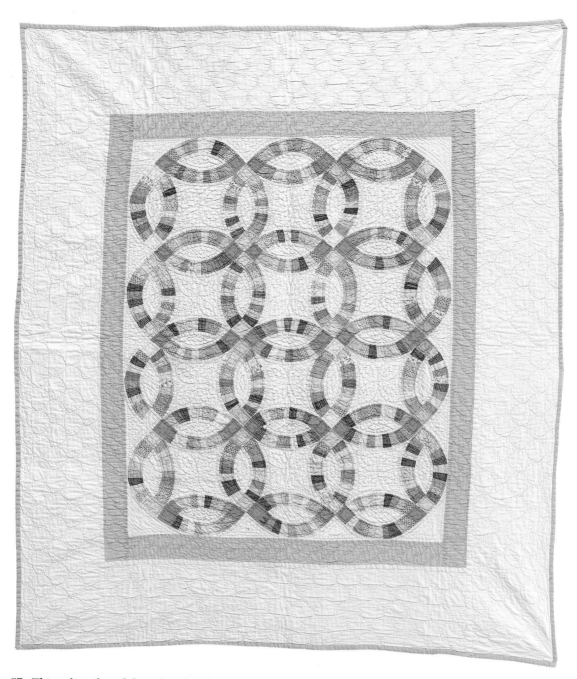

57. This crib quilt in delicately soft colors was made in Honeyville, Indiana, c. 1935 by Anna (Mrs. John A.) Raber, an Amish lady. She appears to have been quite liberal in her beliefs, for she included some scraps of printed fabrics, which are generally considered flamboyant and an affront to the traditional religious beliefs of the Amish. Indiana; c. 1935; 54″ x 49″.

58. The quilt illustrated above was an exciting find for the collection, as I am partial to the color red, and it is used here so beautifully and expertly. Added to that is the wonderful quilting throughout the whole piece, even including some hearts to be found in the border. Michigan; 1935–1945; 81½″ x 81″.

59. Friendship Knot is the name of this variation of the Double Wedding Ring design, and one assumes that the name comes from the half LeMoyne Star motifs that face each other on the four sides of the rings. Compare the soft palette of this example with the rather hard brilliance of the quilt on the opposite page. 1930–1945; 80″ x 72″.

60. Another Friendship Knot quilt is shown here, very different in feeling from the one in figure 58. This piece gives the impression that all was subordinated to the importance of the touching half stars. This pattern was apparently especially popular in the South. 1945–1960; 86″ x 75¼″.

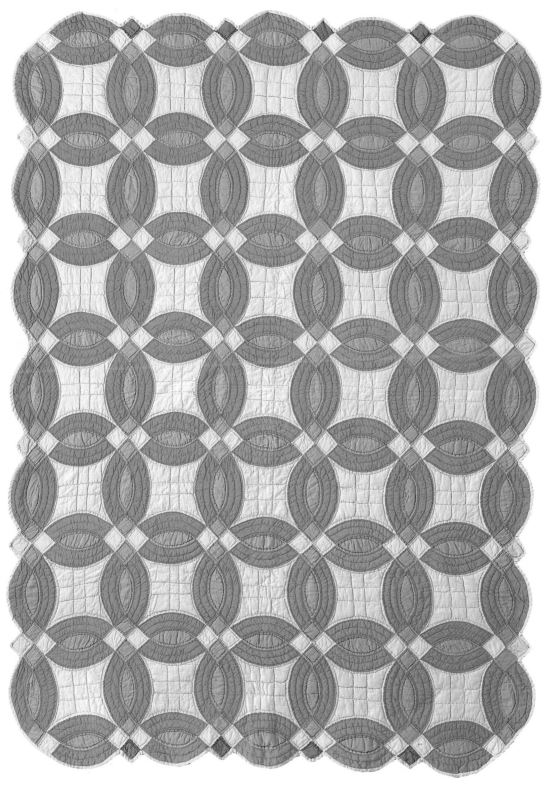

61. Once again we show a Double Wedding Ring made with solid rather than pieced rings. It is instructive to note how the pink patches at the intersections help to tone down the orange-and-green color scheme. The dark green patches at the top and bottom add a nice bit of punctuation. Texas; c. 1935; 85″ x 62″.

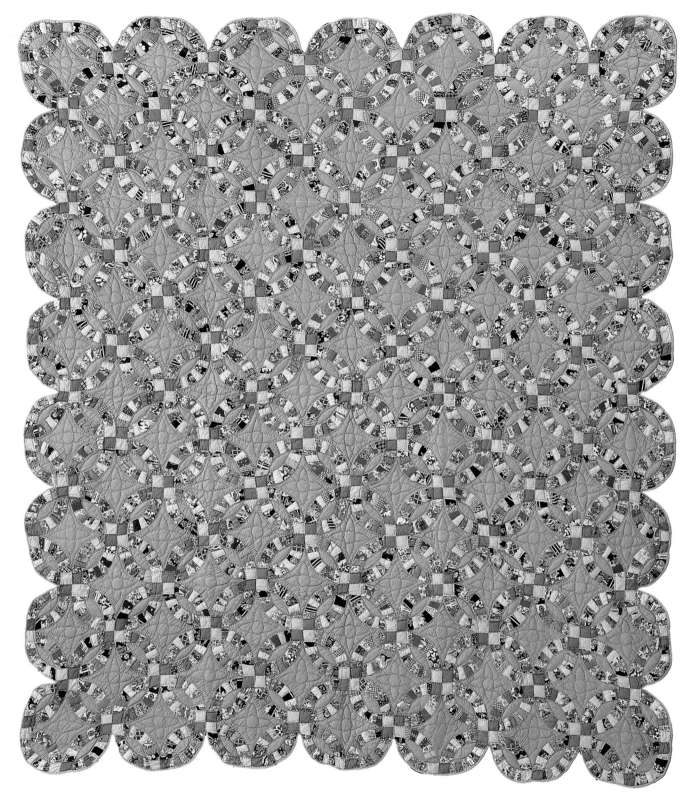

62. Figures 49 and 50 show two other quilts using purple, so it will be interesting to compare them to this eyedazzler that literally explodes with bright color, yet which is nicely held in check by the blue patches that travel through the quilt. 1935–1940; 74″ x 68″.

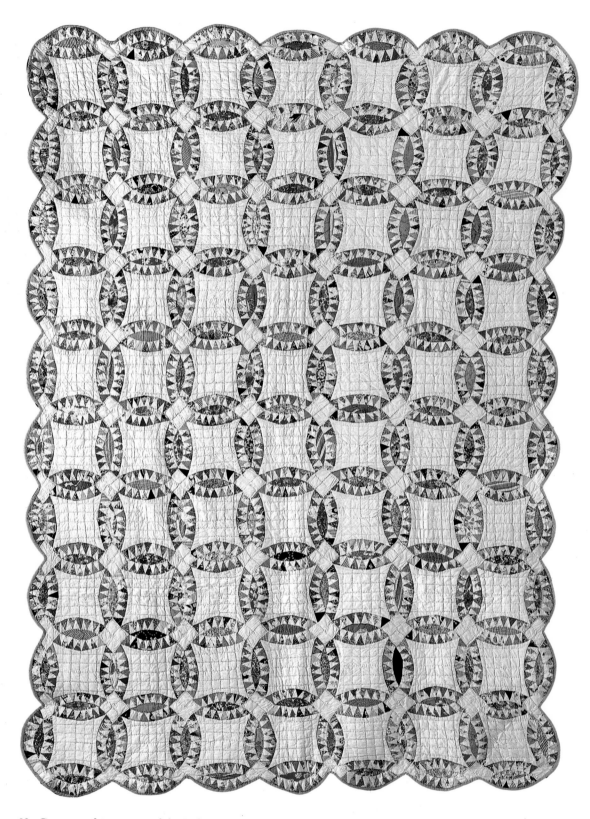

63. Compare this version of the Indian Wedding Ring or Pickle Dish design with that illustrated in figure 19. There the effect is very precise, cool, and collected; in this example all is color and variety and just as interesting. The name Pickle Dish was probably inspired by the cut-glass dishes that became the rage with American homemakers in the late 19th and early 20th centuries. Ohio (perhaps Amish); 1935–1945; 88″ x 62½″.

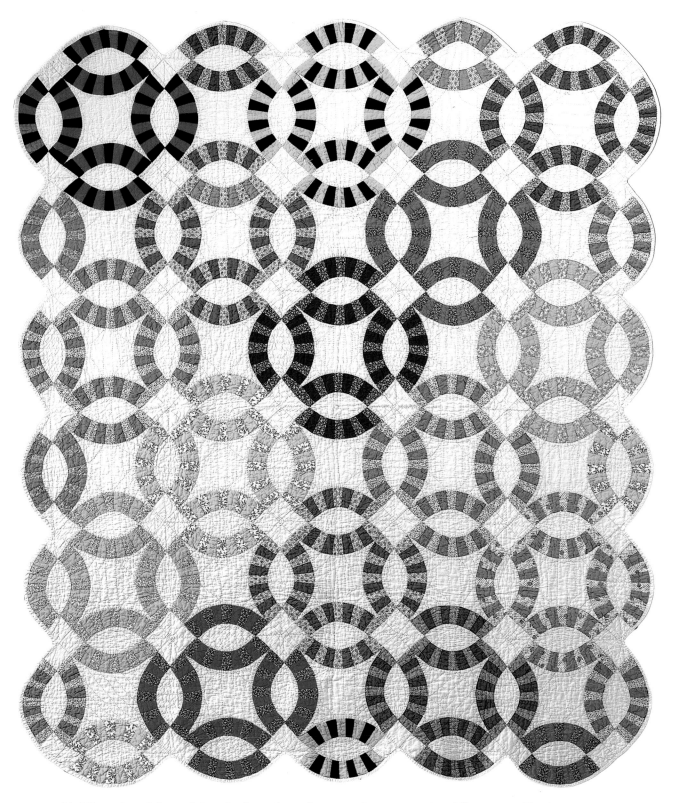

64. The maker of this quilt loved color and was determined to present it in a different way. For the most part, each of the wedding rings is pieced in just one color, but even that scheme is changed here and there to make sure that variety is the spice of quilts, just as it is the spice of life. c. 1935; 75″ x 68″.

PATTERNS AND INSTRUCTIONS
FOR
MAKING A WEDDING RING QUILT

A NOTE ABOUT THE PATTERNS

We have taken some liberties with the patterns reproduced here only because there is always a certain amount of distortion in quilts that have been used and washed. When you start, the pattern should allow you to make all of the circular designs truly circular. In the old quilts this did not always happen—probably because the patterns were cardboard hand-me-downs and the more they were used, the more distorted the circles became. We have tried to stay to the general dimensions and the numbers of pieces but to produce real rings—at least on paper.

GETTING READY TO CREATE

Pre-planning is the key to a perfect quilt. Some quilters believe that at least one-third of the total working time should be spent in planning. This formula will vary greatly, but it is safe to say that you should spend a large amount of time in choosing a pattern, making templates, combining and preparing fabrics, and stitching a test block.

The information given here is pertinent only to Wedding Ring quilts so that there are omissions from these general directions for such varieties as medallion and appliqué quilts. For instance, the patterns are all continuous except for the Friendship Knot which is a true block pattern. There are no sashes and few borders. The continuous piecing process sometimes leads to small changes in the finished quilt size. The clue to accuracy is to be careful every inch of the way. Test the pattern pieces by tracing them together, mark the seam lines, and be sure that you stitch right on the markings. It may be possible for the professional seamstress to piece these patterns on the machine, but in general let's say that they are designed for hand piecing. Before you cut out all the necessary pieces, cut just enough to make up one section and sew it together to get a better idea of the problems involved.

There is no reason to make a quilt in the exact colors—or even the exact size—suggested in the pictures and directions. Three of the quilts shown are made of scrap—a very popular choice for Wedding Rings. Perhaps this idea came from the belief that a young girl should have made several other quilts and most of her clothing by the time she prepared for marriage so the scraps of her life and endeavors up to that time will be preserved in the quilt. Perhaps it was a way of encouraging thrift. It certainly makes for young, bright, happy quilts.

Generous fabric allowance is given in these directions for both planned and scrap quilts. If you cut very carefully, you might even be able to increase the size of your quilt by one row without buying more. There is also the possibility that a fairly new quilter may not cut so carefully or may make an error, and if none of these things happens, there will be leftover fabric for another quilt. Fabric widths vary greatly— from 36 inches to, in rare cases, 54 inches. With all of these things in mind, it is often wise to buy your fabric at a quilt shop where everyone is knowledgeable about such things.

As you select fabrics for these patterns—all of which have many small pieces—you should look for thin to medium weight 100% cottons with a very close weave. Some cotton blends of the same type are suitable. Loose weaves are more apt to ravel and split along the seams and heavy fabrics will be bulky in patterns with such small pieces. Especially in the scrap quilts, a white that is not dead white will blend more smoothly with the multicolors and give a gentler effect. There are numerous highly suitable muslin-colored 100% cotton fabrics available. You might want to buy ⅛-yard pieces of several, mark them with any pertinent information so that you don't get them mixed up, and wash them to see how well they perform. You do not want ones that set in masses of hard wrinkles or those that lose all their life and body or the ones that get stiffer after being wet.

All fabric should be pre-washed before cutting and sewing. The larger pieces can be run through one warm-water rinse and spin in the washer and small ones can be dipped in a basin full of water, allowed to soak through, and hung flat to dry. If you have any doubt about the color stability of darker colors (usually red or navy or purple) lay the wet fabric on an old white towel for ten or fifteen minutes to see whether the color "bleeds." In general, it is best to discard any fabric that runs before combining it with white and lighter colors that it may ultimately ruin. If you have bought a large piece of this fabric and feel dedicated to using it, there are ways of making it safe or at least safer. Simply running it twice through the washing machine may do the trick. If the "bleeding" is very bad, try soaking the fabric in a fairly strong solution of cold water and white vinegar—about two cups of vinegar to a basin of water. If the vinegar isn't handy, you may use cold salted water. Either process acts as a mordant to set the dye. Rinse the fabric thoroughly after using either of these mixtures and test it again on a white towel. If it still "bleeds," discard it no matter how much you love it!

The grain or thread line of the fabric should be straight—that is, the cross line should be exactly perpendicular to the length line. On print fabrics it is easier to see the grain on the reverse side. If it does not seem straight, it can be pulled and corrected while the fabric is still damp. To make sure that you have the grain really square, press it after straightening it, while holding it in shape.

Choosing batting is difficult for a beginner. If you feel uncertain about your needs, consult your local quilt shop or quilting teacher. Of course, each person has a different idea of what the finished quilt should look like. When choosing batting for a quilt in which appearance matters more than warmth, try a thinner batting—all cotton or cotton and polyester. The many seams in the Wedding Ring quilts will make heavy battings awkward.

The backing fabric is most often the same as one of the fabrics used in the top, thus affording a perfectly compatible texture and weight. Cotton-blend fabrics with a lot of chemical finish are not easy to quilt through and are sometimes stiff, so are quite unsuitable for backing. Most no-iron sheets fall into this group, so you may as well give up on the idea of a seamless back unless you can find really old-fashioned all-cotton sheets and wash them until they are very soft. Resign yourself to the idea that there will be at least one seam in the quilt back.

Pins, needles, and thread are all necessary and very much an individual choice, as are the larger tools like scissors, sewing machines and cutting surfaces. The best advice on all of these items is to choose only the finest equipment and then to treat it in the way that you'd expect any professional craftsman to do. For instance, no one except you should ever use your scissors—and only for fabric! Pins should be in a closed box and any bent or dull ones should be discarded. Needles will last forever without rusting if kept in a little needle case with wool pages—the lanolin in the wool protects the steel.

In choosing your equipment, ask the people who quilt well what they prefer. Most will tell you that a short needle—called a "between"—is best and the smaller the size or thickness, the better. As the size numbers increase, the dimension of the needle gets smaller so that a 12 is much finer than a 7. Most people find that an 8 to 10 is easiest to use and still possible to thread. Quilting is a demanding task and you will find a thimble a necessity.

Two kinds of pins are used in quilting, a fine "silk" pin for holding pieces together as they are being seamed and a large-headed pin to go through all the layers when the batting and backing are being put in place with the top, preparatory to quilting.

All-cotton thread is usually recommended for quilting, but again there are varieties to try. The ones that work best are not necessarily sold as quilting thread.

For most quilters basting the layers together preparatory to quilting is a necessity and we will stay with that idea, although we admit you may learn other ways as you go along. A frame of some type is usually best for smooth quilting. It may be a large ratchet frame or four "stout sticks" held together with C-clamps at the corners. There are now many frames on the market that offer solutions to small space, including one made of a sort of plastic pipe. You may also prefer the more mobile lap frames or hoops. Check out the market to see what is available and get demonstrations of the ones that you don't understand. Ask quilting friends and instructors—get a knowledgeable friend to help you set up a quilt for the final quilting.

MAKING AND USING PATTERNS

All patterns in this book are given *without seam allowances* to assure accuracy in piecing. As you will probably be stitching by hand it is important to mark the seamlines with light pencil on the reverse of the fabric pieces and then cut the extra ¼-inch seam allowance by eye. At first you may need to measure and mark the cutting line every so often, but your eye will soon get trained.

Because you will mark many times around each pattern piece, the pieces will need to be made of a very firm material. The best pattern material is a thin translucent plastic made for stencils and available in all art and some stationery stores. Using a fine pencil and a ruler and artists' curves, trace the pieces accurately from the pages of the book. Cut exactly on the lines, using small sharp scissors or a stencil knife. Some quilters like to trace the patterns onto ordinary typewriter paper and then glue it to the smooth side of sandpaper so that the rough side can be placed against the back of the fabric to hold it firmly as you draw around the stencil or template, as it is usually called in quilting.

Remember: as you place the templates on the back of the fabric and draw around them there must be two seam-allowance widths left between each template—that is ½ inch for two ¼-inch seam allowances. Be careful to lay the pieces so that the grain line is as you want it to be. The marked grain lines on the pattern pieces are suggestions only, so you are free to change them if you want special effects with plaids or stripes. (Note the use of the stripe in the *Indian Wedding Ring*.)

The small motifs for quilting can almost all be made in the same stiff material as the piecing patterns. The Spider Web pattern in the Indian Wedding Ring will not work in this way, so it should be drawn with dark lines on firm paper and used under the fabric on a light box. The design can then be traced with a #3 pencil or other very light marker. The main point of marking is that it be barely dark enough to see for stitching and either removable or too light to see after the stitching is completed. Art gum eraser will remove some traces of regular pencil without damage to the fabric. Most of the quilting on the Wedding Rings is simple outline that needs no marking.

It is probably helpful to mention that simple light boxes are available at many art stores and will be of great use to a dedicated quilter or needleworker. If you're not sure you'll ever use one again, you can make the simplest kind by suspending a piece of heavy glass between two piles of books about 4 inches from your working surface. Lay a small light bulb on a cord under the glass (15 watts will do). Tape the paper pattern on top of the glass and lay the cloth over it. Trace with a #3 pencil or any chosen washable pen. (Be sure to test any marker that you choose and to ask the advice of other quilters.)

PIECING THE WEDDING RING

Set aside a lot of winter evenings for cutting the many tiny pieces that are necessary for any Wedding Ring quilt. You may find ways of cutting in multilayers that will work for you, but you will still have to mark those seam lines on each and every piece! You may find it helpful to mark plastic bags for all the like pieces, #1, #2, etc., and keep the cut and marked pieces filed in this way.

As it seems most practical to join these pieces by hand, the directions will be given without reference to machine piecing. All pieces will be placed with right sides together. Pin the seam lines together carefully, working from each end so that the corners meet exactly. If you use the fine silk pins and pin the ends, checking through to both sides, then pin the space between, with all pins perpendicular to the seam line

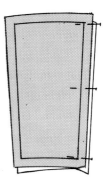

and taking up only a small amount of fabric, you can sew by hand with a running stitch exactly on the marked line. Use a small neat knot in the thread and take one backstitch at the start and one or two more at the end. When sewing by hand, there is no need to sew off the raw edges; start and stop the stitching right on the penciled line, leaving the seams free at the ends.

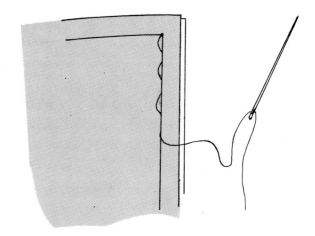

Decide how you want to assemble the motifs—usually piecing together the smallest segments that form strips, arcs, stars, or Nine-Patch formations first. Build up a larger unit and then join these with the pieces that logically fall between. Press the seams to one side as you go, trying always to fold the seams toward the darkest fabric. If this is not possible, you may go back and trim out any dark edges that show through the white.

The straight borders should be cut after the entire top is pieced and pressed so that any changes that occur in size can be taken into account. Most of the quilts shown have what is generally called an Amish border—that is to say with straight joins at the corners rather than a miter. The two end strips will be sewn in place, the seams pressed and then the two side pieces added.

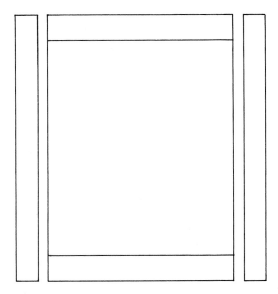

If you choose to miter the corners of a border, there is a simple way of figuring the lengths and making a perfectly diagonal miter. Cut both side and end borders to the total desired finished length of the quilt edges. On the reverse side of each piece draw a square box in the corner, leaving the seam allowance outside—a 3-inch box for a 3-inch wide border or a 4-inch box for a 4-inch wide border. Mark a cross from corner to corner of each box. Pin and seam the borders to ends and sides, matching the corner of the boxes with the corner of the pieced area of the quilt. This leaves the square boxes free. Match the diagonal lines in each pair

of corner boxes so that the border lies flat, then pin and stitch these lines. Trim off the excess and press the seams. The top is now ready to layer and quilt.

QUILTING

The designs for quilting must be marked as described above. The seams must be carefully pressed and trimmed where necessary as described above. The top should be smooth and flat and ready to quilt.

Trim all selvages off the backing fabric as they are heavy to stitch through and can shrink and cause distortion in the finished quilt. Cut the backing so that the finished piece will be slightly larger, two inches or so, than the finished top. You may make one seam down the center back, or two seams to form a panel in the center, or the seams may run crosswise of the back. Press the backing perfectly smooth.

Lay the backing right side down on a large flat surface—probably the floor and preferably without a carpet. Smooth the batting gently over the backing without stretching it. Trim it to match the backing. Lay the top wrong side down on the batting. Pin and then baste lengthwise, crosswise, and diagonally out to the corners.

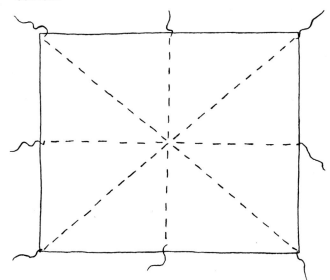

The matter of quilting with or without a frame or of using a lap frame or a standing frame must be decided by each individual on the basis of space and time. If you find it convenient to quilt in odd hours in front of the television or at a friend's house, you will find lap-quilting without a frame or with a small portable frame your best bet. If you have the space for a large frame, there is a certain professionalism and the joy of seeing the quilt in progress in the frame that are appealing. The large standing frame also accommodates more than one quilter.

Each frame has its own specifications for "putting in" the quilt. On large frames the quilt is generally attached with stitching to fabric wrapped on the rods along the sides. At its simplest, this large frame is what Ruth Finley (in *Old Patchwork Quilts and the Women Who Made Them*, 1929) calls "four stout sticks" pegged or clamped together and set up on chair backs or sawhorses for use. There are smaller lap versions of this same type of frame and there are hoop frames—both standing and lap size—that work exactly like large embroidery hoops. If you want to dispense with frames altogether, you will have to baste more so that there is no slippage in the layers.

The stitch for quilting is the simplest of running stitches—the trick is in keeping it as even as possible, on both the top and bottom. The knot must be made large enough to hold, but small enough so that it will slip through the weave of the backing and hide itself in the batting. One way of making this happen is by running the needle in on a slant and giving the knot a slight tug, just enough to pull it through the backing fabric. As you start the running stitch, you may take a small backstitch to keep the knot from traveling out through the top layer. The end can be fastened with a backstitch and then the thread run for an inch or so between the layers before being cut off.

The outline quilting is best worked about ⅛ inch from the seam lines. Try a sample line and see whether it looks better even a little farther away from the seam itself. This depends to some degree on how heavy the fabric is and how many seams there are. The open spaces can be filled with the designs given or any appropriate design that you prefer.

BINDING

There are a number of ways to finish the edges of a quilt. The classic Double Wedding Ring has a scalloped edge which can only be finished with a narrow bias binding. As this type also makes a very good finish for any edge, it is the only one we will deal with here.

Cutting bias is easiest if there is a large enough piece of fabric to lay out a square with the selvage still on one edge. Fold the piece so that the cross grain lies exactly

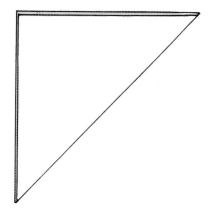

on the length grain or selvage. Crease the fold. With a yardstick mark along the fold on the wrong side of the fabric. Measure and mark parallel lines as far apart as the desired width of the bias, usually about 1¼ to 1½

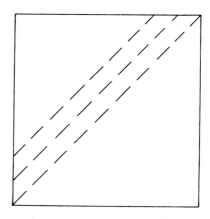

inches. Cut the strips along the marked lines. Lay the right sides together so that they can be seamed along the grain—either length or cross—and pin. Stitch the pieces together with a ¼-inch seam and press the seams open flat. If you have cut the binding 1½ inches wide,

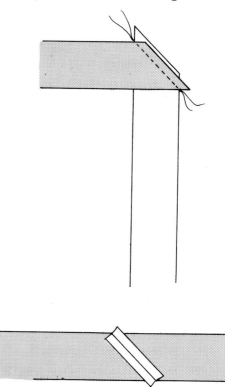

you should have a finished binding of ⅜ inches—always figure four times the desired finished width when cutting.

To ascertain the exact amount of bias binding needed for the straight-sided, quilts (not the classic Double Wedding Ring) measure the quilted piece across the center on both the length and width. You will then need two widths and two lengths, plus a little bit for finishing the ends. *Note:* quilting shrinks the original flat measurement so that you may see a slight ripple in the edge. You may want to run a long basting stitch about ½ inch from the raw edge of the top and ease this fullness in to match the measurements you have just taken. You may now trim the batting and backing to match the top.

The scalloped edge of the Double Wedding Ring presents special problems, even in measuring. There is no exact way to measure, but it is safe to add about one third to the amount of twice the length and twice the width used for a quilt with straight sides. Prepare the edge as you would any other quilt, basting the layers together and trimming the backing and batting.

Lay the binding right side down to the right side of the quilt top, with raw edges matching and cross pin it in place without stretching it. Stitch a seam one quarter of the binding width from the edge (⅜ inch for an 1½ inch binding). The corners of the straight-edged quilts and the points on the Double Wedding Ring require special treatment. Stop the stitching a seam-allowance

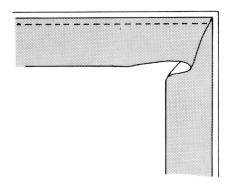

point. At the indentations on the scalloped edge, simply pivot the stitching with no extra pleat of fabric. At the point where the ends join, fold one end under and lay the other end on top of it, so that when it is turned over all raw ends will be concealed.

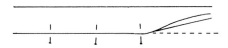

Fold the binding over hard against the stitching—press gently if desired—and then fold it over the edge. You should have about one quarter of the width left to turn under on the back side with the turned edge

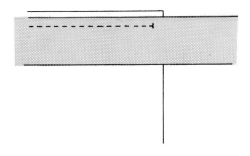

width from the corner and secure the stitching. Fold a small pleat in the binding, allowing it to turn the corner easily. Start stitching along the next side at the same

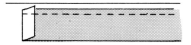

exactly touching the first stitching. Pin the folded edge in place and sew it with a blind stitch so that it remains smooth and even all along on both sides.

The only tricks to bias binding are in the handling. Be sure that it is completely filled with the quilt edge when you turn it over. Be sure not to pull or stretch it at any time—it is very easy to distort bias. On the Double Wedding Ring binding a nice pleat should form in the indentations and the points. It is all a matter of handling.

Diagram of quilt illustrated in figure 14

Note: We have taken liberties with the old-fashioned Double Wedding Ring to make it conform to today's standards for a true circle. There is also a larger piece (#6) given so that the arcs may be made up of seven pieces instead of twelve.

Dimensions: 71 x 90 inches.

Materials: all 45-inch fabrics.
    6½ yards white—includes backing
    1½ yards light blue—includes bias binding
    1 yard bright pink
    2 yards (approximately) scrap—some may be the pink and blue

Cut: Add ¼-inch seam allowance all around each piece and to each measurement given.

For each complete circle: (The circles interlock so that it is necessary to make some partial circles)
    1 white #1
    4 pink #2

    8 arcs of:
        10 scrap #4   *then*
            or   4 blue #5
        5 scrap #6   4 blue #5 reversed

Directions: Piece eight arcs of #4 and #5 (or #5 and #6) pieces. Seam these to each side of the #2 pieces and seam the #3 pieces in the ends. Join the four completed "melon" shapes around the sides of a #1 piece. Make more complete circles and join them with more of the completed "melons" and white #1 pieces, as shown.

Quilt the center designs in the #1 and #2 pieces and outline quilt the other pieces as you like. Finish with a narrow bias binding, being careful to ease it around the curves and miter at the indentations and points.

CLASSIC DOUBLE WEDDING RING
(*as illustrated*)

Note: If you want to make an old-fashioned looking quilt, as shown in figure 14, you should use pieces 1a, 2a, 3a, 4a, 5a, or the alternate 6a and the same directions as for the true-circle version.

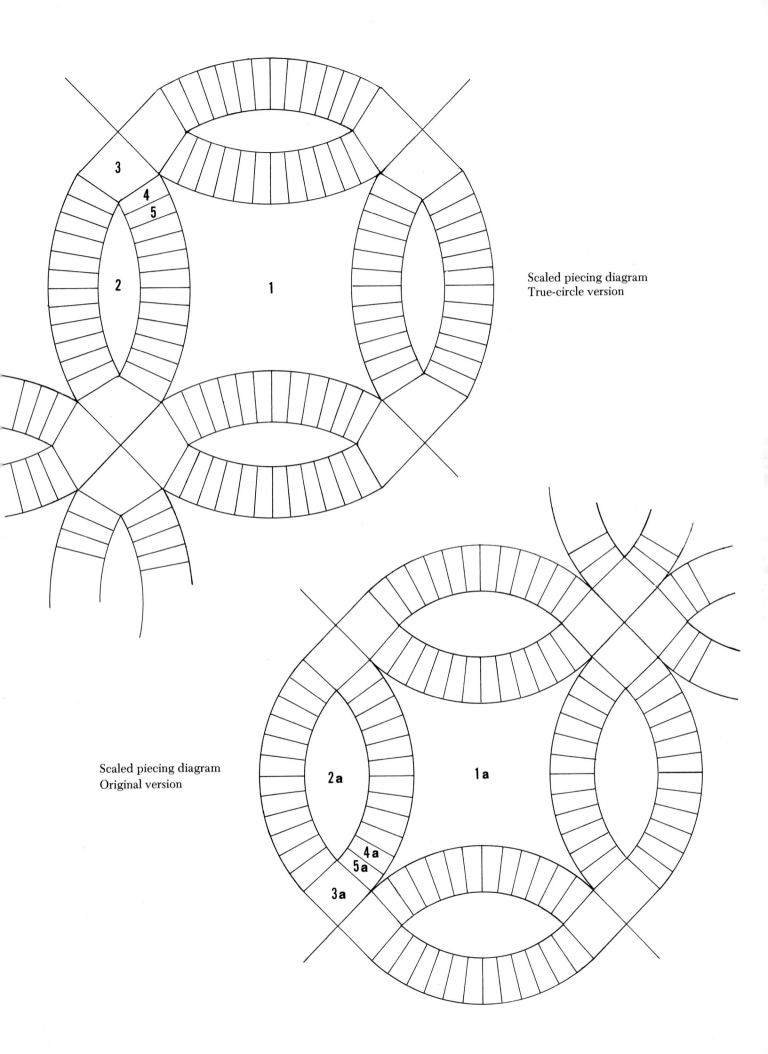

Scaled piecing diagram
True-circle version

Scaled piecing diagram
Original version

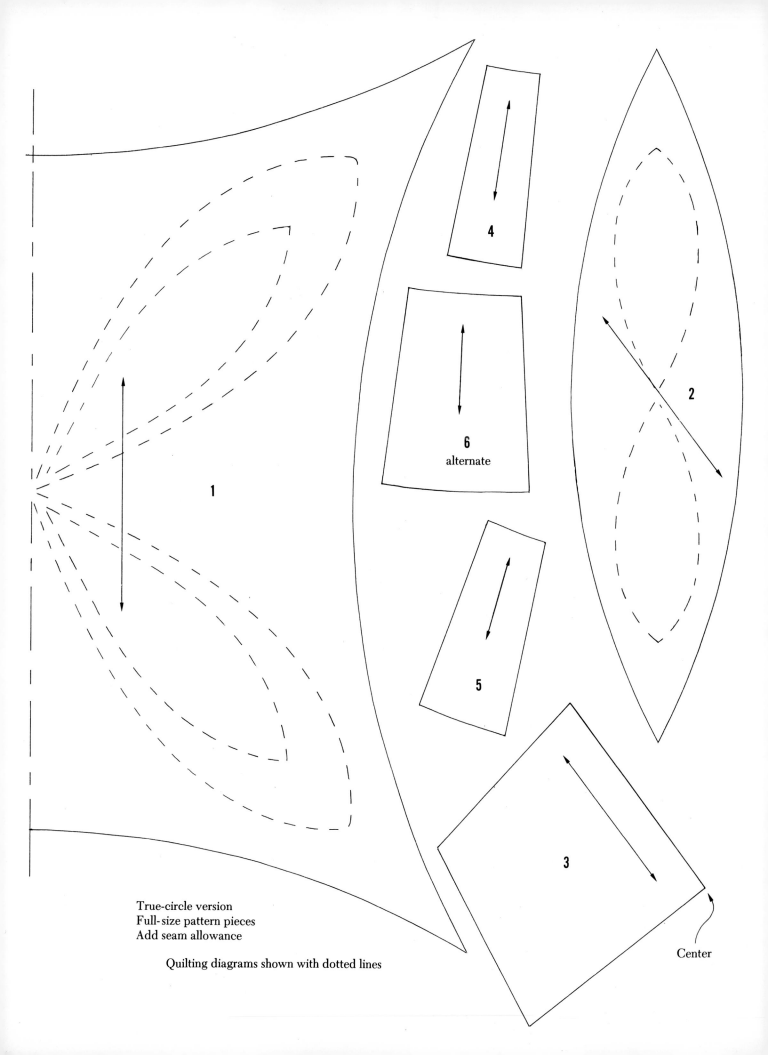

4

6

alternate

2

5

1

3

Center

True-circle version
Full-size pattern pieces
Add seam allowance

Quilting diagrams shown with dotted lines

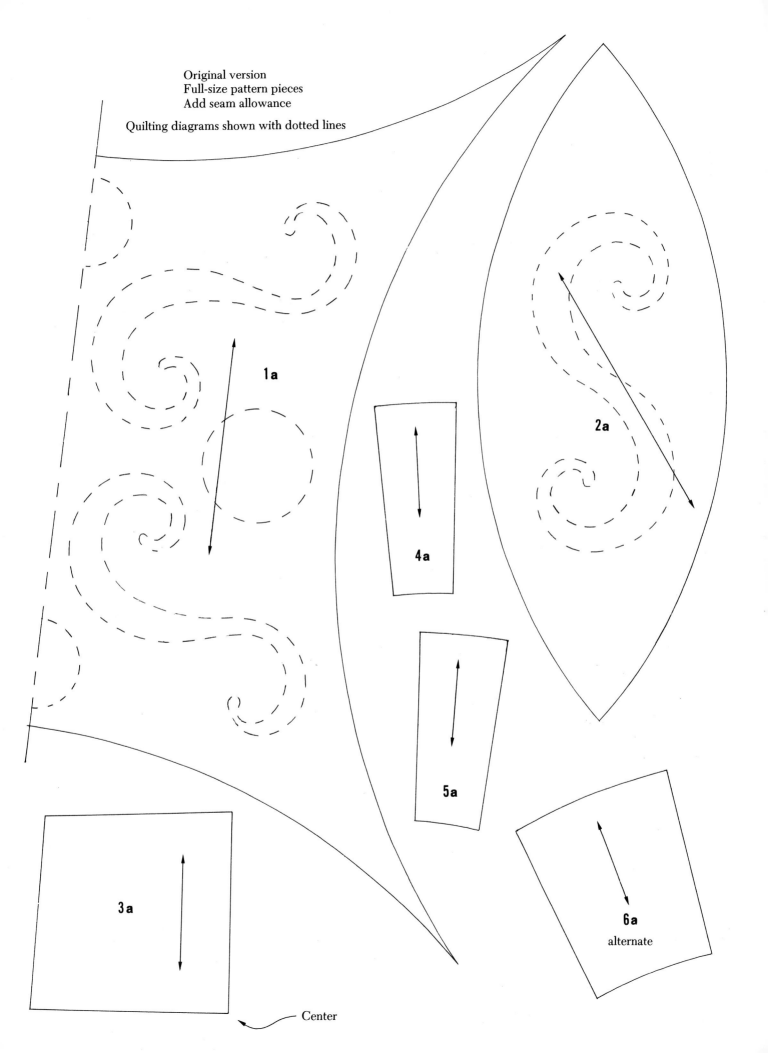

Original version
Full-size pattern pieces
Add seam allowance

Quilting diagrams shown with dotted lines

1a

2a

4a

5a

3 a

6a

alternate

Center

Diagram of quilt illustrated in figure 19

INDIAN WEDDING RING
or
PICKLE DISH

Dimensions: 73 x 91½ inches.

Materials: all 45-inch fabrics.
   9   yards white—includes backing and binding
   3   yards solid blue (can be mixed shades)
   1½ yards blue-and-white pin stripe

Cut: Add ¼-inch seam allowance all around each piece and to each measurement given.

For each ring: (Total of 12 rings)
1 white #1	8 blue #6
4 striped #2	8 white #7
20 white #3	8 blue #8
8 blue #4	8 white #9
8 blue #5	

For center fillers:
   6 white #1

For side fillers:
   4 white one-fourth #1
  10 white one-half #1

For side borders:
  88 blue #10
  86 white #10
   4 white one-half #10

For borders:
  2 blue strips, ends, 69½ x 1¾ inches
  2 blue strips, sides, 91½ x 1¾ inches

Directions: Piece each blue-and-white curved saw-tooth section. Join one onto each side of the striped "melon" piece. Join the #9 pieces into the ends. Join one "melon" onto each side of each #1 piece to make a complete ring. Make four rows of three each rings, using the extra #1 pieces between. Fill in the sides to make a rectangle.

Piece the sawtoogh borders for the sides and join them to the center rectangle. Add the blue end borders and then the side borders.

Use outline quilting around each piece. Quilt the spider web in the large #1 pieces. Finish the edge with narrow white binding.

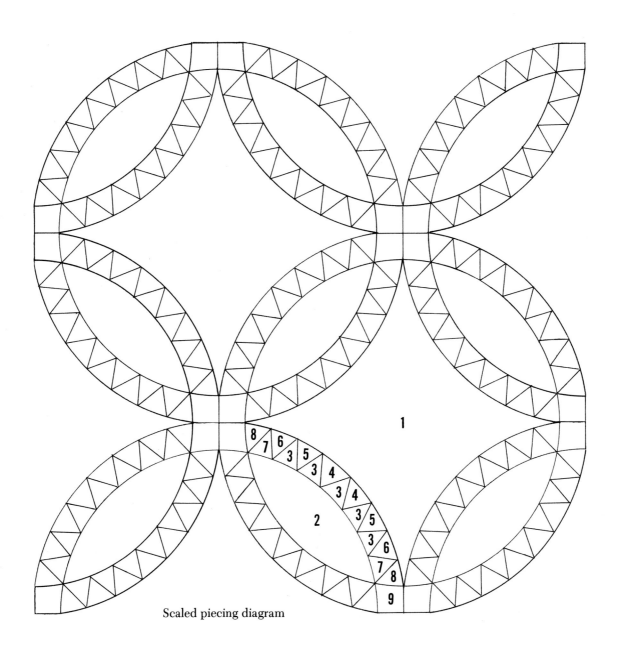

Scaled piecing diagram

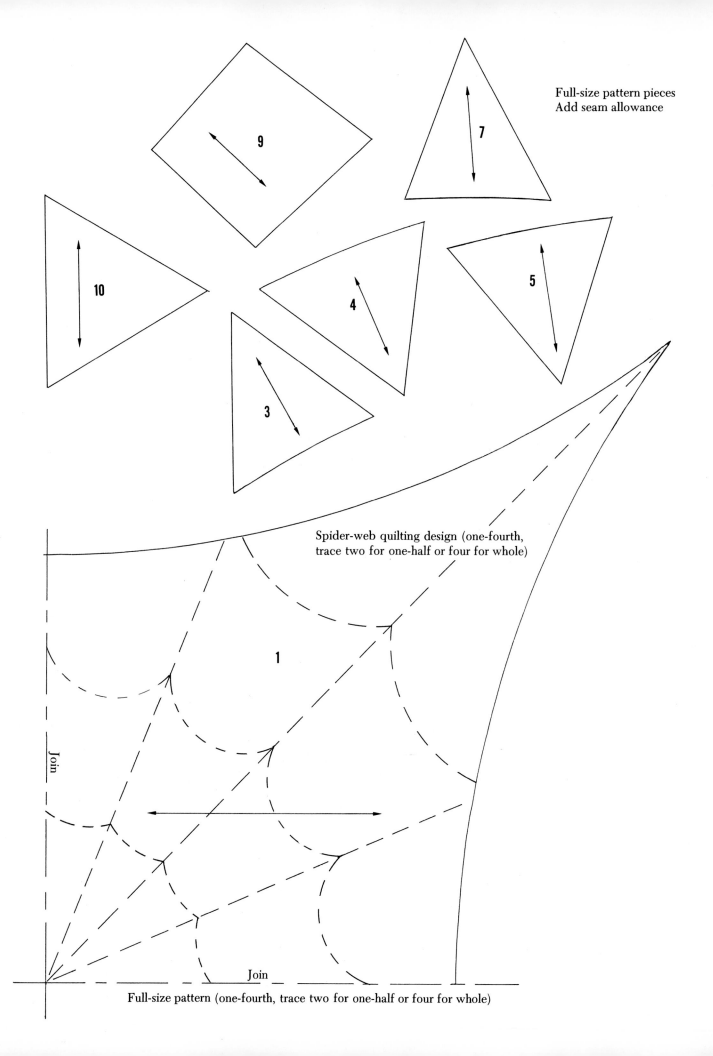

Full-size pattern pieces
Add seam allowance

9

7

10

4

5

3

Spider-web quilting design (one-fourth,
trace two for one-half or four for whole)

1

Join

Join

Full-size pattern (one-fourth, trace two for one-half or four for whole)

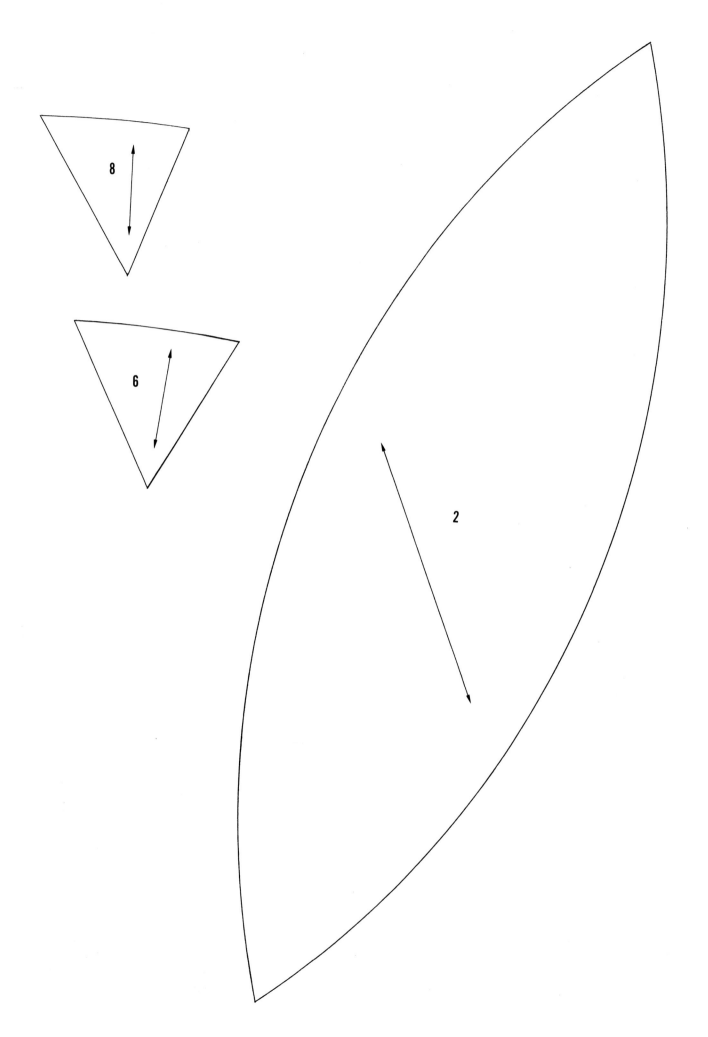

8

6

2

GOLDEN WEDDING RING

Diagram of quilt illustrated
in figure 28

Note: We have given two versions of this elaborate pattern, hoping to simplify its construction for those who feel daunted by the original. The #1 and #2 pieces forming the center Star are replaced by a gently curved assembly of #10 and #11. The #6 and #7 have been replaced by one #9 piece.

Dimensions: 76 x 84½ inches.

Materials: all 45-inch fabrics.
   7 yards white—includes backing
   3 yards blue—includes bias binding
   2 yards bright yellow

Cut: Add ¼-inch seam allowance all around each piece and to each measurement given.

For each center design: (Total of 23 centers, 18½ inches, point to point).
   6 yellow #1
   6 blue #2
      or
   1 yellow #10
   6 blue #11   (see note)
      then
   6 white #3
   6 yellow #4
   6 blue #5
   6 blue #5 reversed
   6 yellow #8

To join:
   1 white #6   *or*
   2 white #7   1 white #9 (see note above)
For ends:
   4 white #10

Directions: If using the original 6-point Star, be sure that you mark the long and short sides of the #1 pieces—*long sides go toward the center.* If you have trouble with the center joinings of Stars, you will find that the #10 and #11 pieces are easier to work with than the original. The other alternative, #6 and #7 replaced by #9, simply reduces the number of pieces to be cut and makes a more continuous assembly with #4, #5, #8 and #9, as opposed to a unit assembly with #6 joined to #4 and #5, then #7 and #8 joined into a curved triangle.

When all twenty-three centers have been joined together, add the four #12 white pieces, two at each end, as shown in the scaled piecing diagram for the ends (a simplification of the original). The four arcs at the ends are finished with a yellow #4, blue #5 and blue #5 reversed, two yellow #8 and a white #13 and white #13 reversed. Join side circles with white #7 pieces.

Use outline quilting around each piece. The three quilting designs given fit exactly into the white areas. Finish the edge with narrow blue binding, being careful to ease it around the curves and miter it in the indentations.

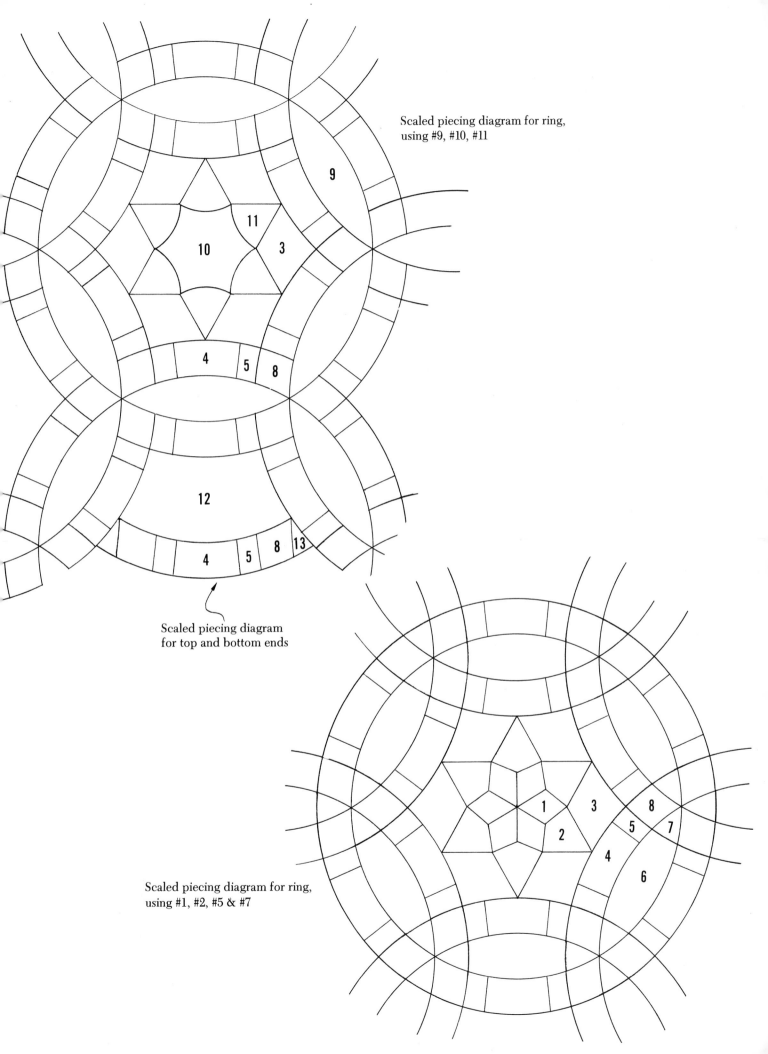

Scaled piecing diagram for ring,
using #9, #10, #11

Scaled piecing diagram
for top and bottom ends

Scaled piecing diagram for ring,
using #1, #2, #5 & #7

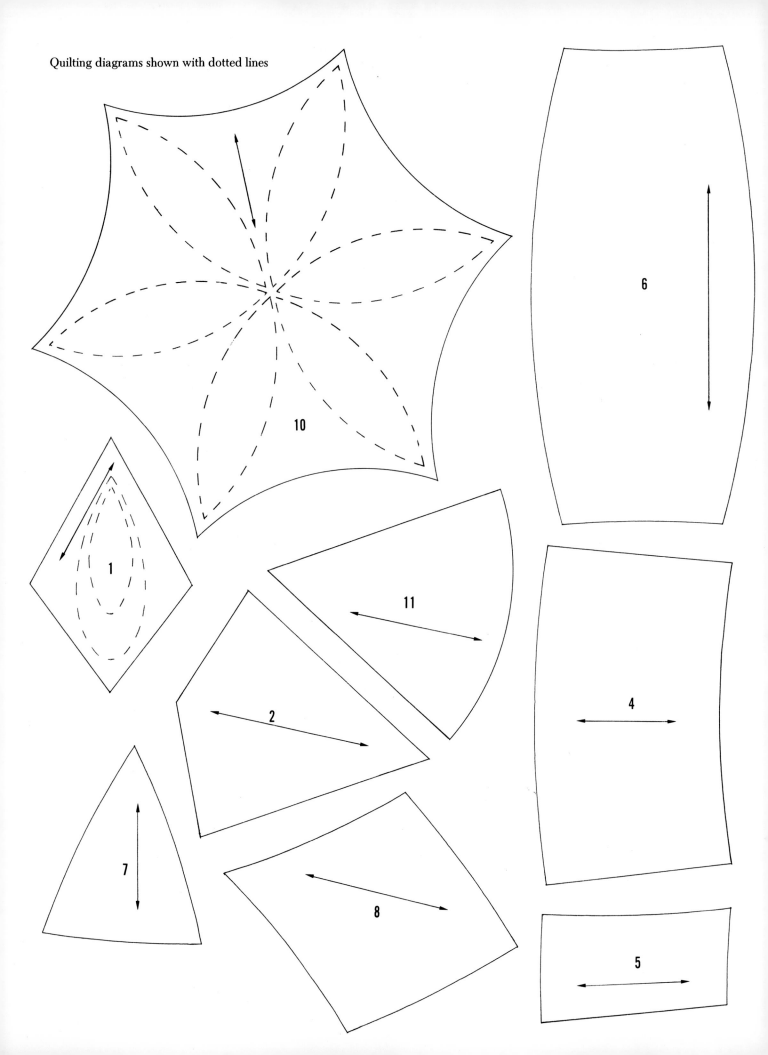

Quilting diagrams shown with dotted lines

10

6

1

11

2

4

7

8

5

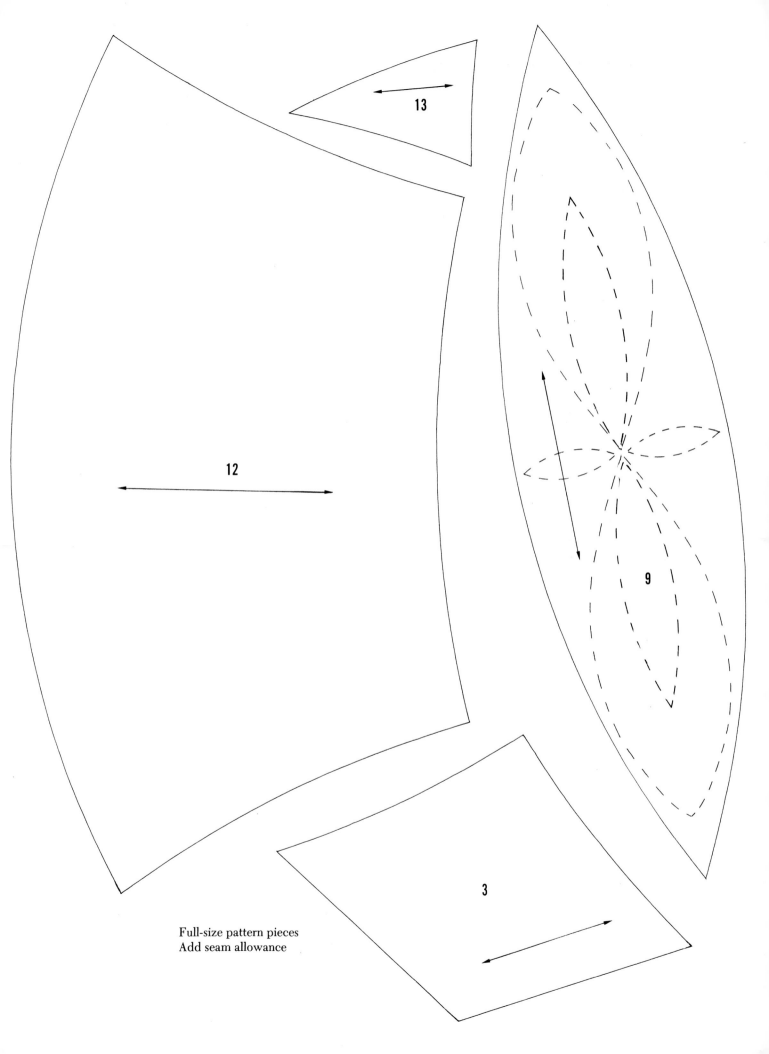

13

12

9

3

Full-size pattern pieces
Add seam allowance

Diagram of quilt illustrated in figure 56

AMISH NINE-PATCH WEDDING RING

Dimensions: 82½ x 99 inches.

Materials: all 45-inch fabrics.
   9½ yards white—includes backing and binding
   3   yards pink
   1½ yards (approximately) scrap in solid colors

Cut: Add ¼-inch seam allowance all around each piece and to each measurement given.

For each complete hexagon: (The forms interlock so that it is possible to make one row across and then to build on that row)
   1   white #1
   6   scrap #2
  24 white #3
  30 scrap #3

For edge fillers:
  White #4
  White #4 reversed
  White #5
  White #6

White #6, reversed
White #7

For borders:
  2 pink strips, ends, 56½ x 4½ inches
  2 pink strips, sides, 82 x 4½ inches
  2 white strips, ends, 65½ x 4 inches
  2 white strips, sides, 90 x 4 inches
  2 pink strips, ends, 73½ x 4½ inches
  2 pink strips, sides, 99 x 4½ inches

Directions: Piece the Nine-Patch sections of five colored squares and four white each. Join these with white hexagons and triangles continuously to form a center piece 56½ x 73 inches. Fill the side areas with the #4, #5, #6 and #7 pieces to form a 56½ x 73 inch rectangular center. Join pink borders to each end, then to each side, then white, and last pink again.

You may outline quilt the hexagon and triangles, but it may be easier in the Nine-Patch to quilt five diagonal rows each way. Use the sunflower design in the center of each hexagon.

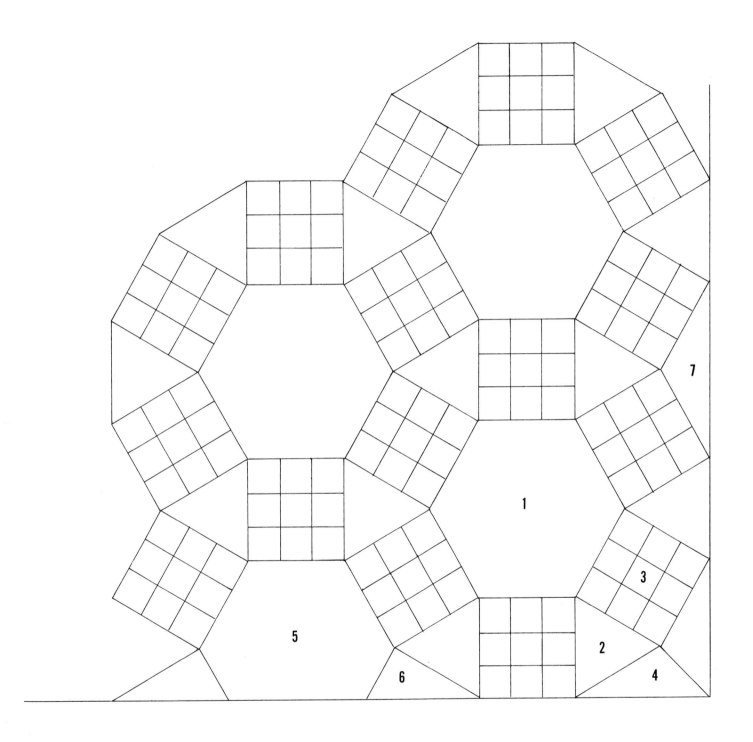

Scaled piecing diagram, lower right hand corner

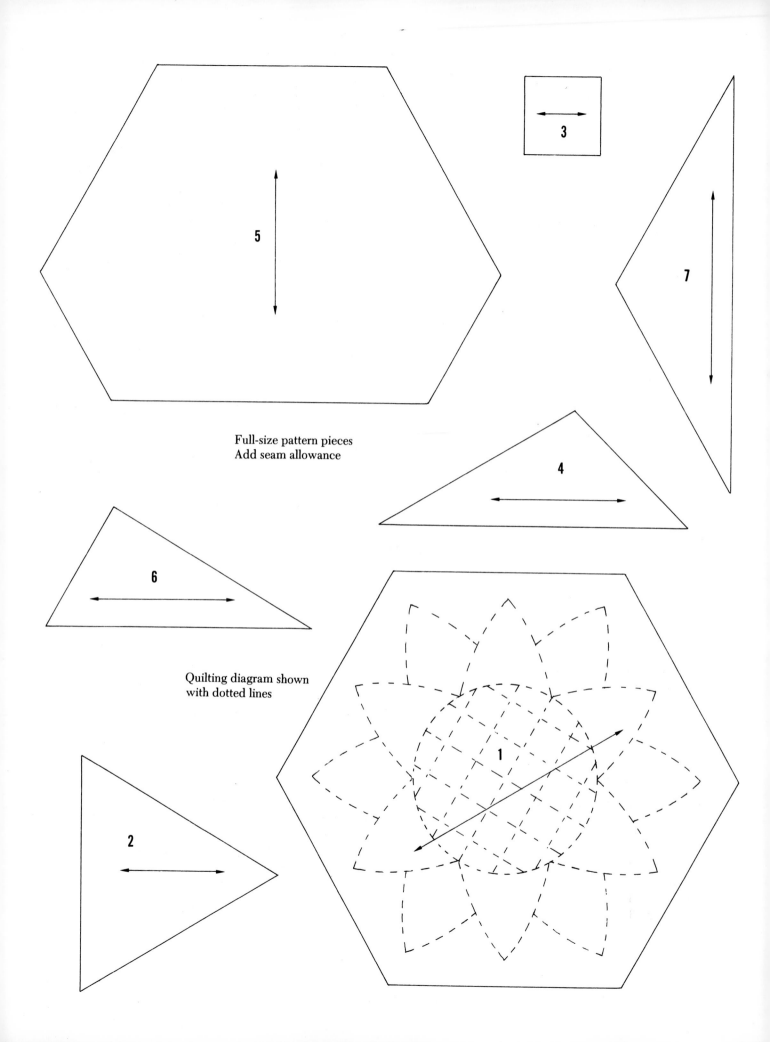

Full-size pattern pieces
Add seam allowance

Quilting diagram shown
with dotted lines

FRIENDSHIP KNOT

Diagram of quilt illustrated in figure 60

Dimensions: 73 x 83½

Materials: all 45-inch fabrics.
  8 yards white—includes backing and binding
  2½ yards black
  1½ yards (approximately) scraps in bright prints and
     solids

*Cut: Add ¼-inch seam allowance all around each piece
and to each measurement given.*

For each block: (total of 42 blocks, 10½ x 10½ inches)
  1 white #1
  4 white #2
  4 white #3
  4 white #3, reversed
  4 white #4
  16 black #5
  4 scrap #6

  4 scrap #6, reversed
  4 scrap #7
  4 scrap #7, reversed

For borders:
  2 black strips, ends 63 x 2¼ inches
  2 black strips, sides, 78 x 2¼ inches
  2 white strips, ends, 67½ x 2¾ inches
  2 white strips, sides, 83½ x 2¾ inches

Directions: Piece the blocks. Join them in six strips of
seven blocks each. Join black border to each end, then
black border to each side. Finish with white end
borders, then white sides.

The original quilt is quilted with a cross-hatch design
in vertical and diagonal lines. There is also the option of
using outline quilting around all the pieces and the
curved designs given for the #1 and #2 pieces. Finish
the edges with narrow white binding.

79

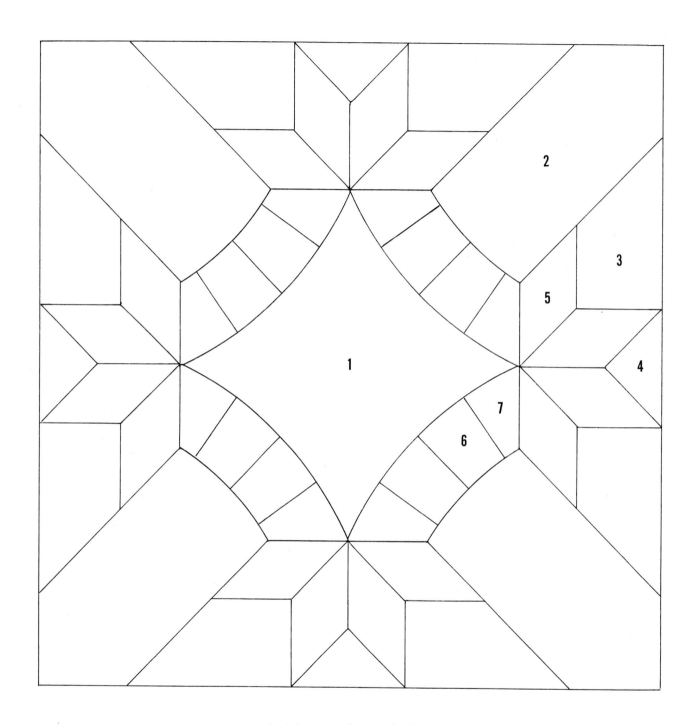

Scaled piecing diagram for block

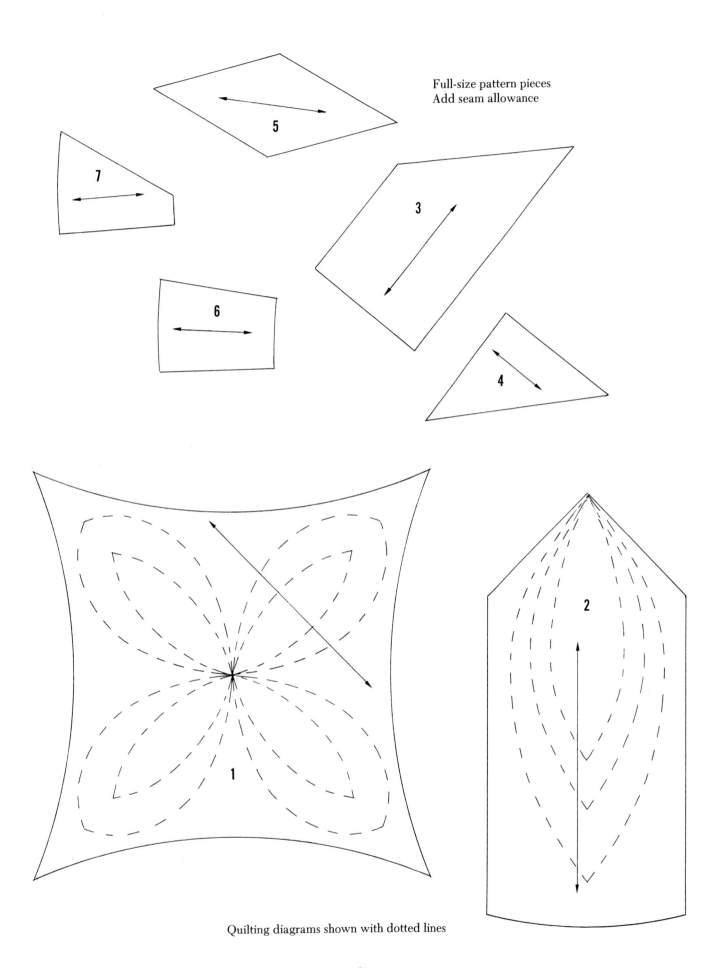

Full-size pattern pieces
Add seam allowance

Quilting diagrams shown with dotted lines

WEDDING RING
BOUQUET
(*Bonus Pattern*)

Dimensions: 79 x 79 inches.

Materials: all 45-inch fabrics.
- 5 yards white—includes bias binding
- 4½ yards pink—includes border and backing
- 3 yards (approximately) scraps in bright pastels, solids, florals, checks, etc.

Cut: Add ¼-inch seam allowance all around each piece and to each measurement given.

For each motif: (excluding #2 joining piece)
- 1 white #1
- 2 scrap #3
- 2 scrap #3 reversed
- 2 scrap #4
- 2 scrap #4 reversed
- 2 scrap #5
- 2 scrap #5 reversed
- 2 scrap #6
- 2 scrap #6 reversed
- 2 scrap #7
- 2 scrap #7 reversed

For borders:
- 2 pink strips, 2½ x 74 inches
- 2 pink strips, 2½ x 79 inches

Directions: Piece the four sides of each motif—pieces #3 through #7—and join them to the sides of the large #1 piece. When an adequate number of these motifs are made, join them together with the white #2 pieces. Use the half #1 pieces (cut with the dotted line for the straight edge) to finish the edges. Seam the two shorter border strips along two sides and the longer ones to the two ends.

Use outline quilting all around each piece and quilt the floral design in the center of the #1 pieces. Finish the quilt with narrow white binding.

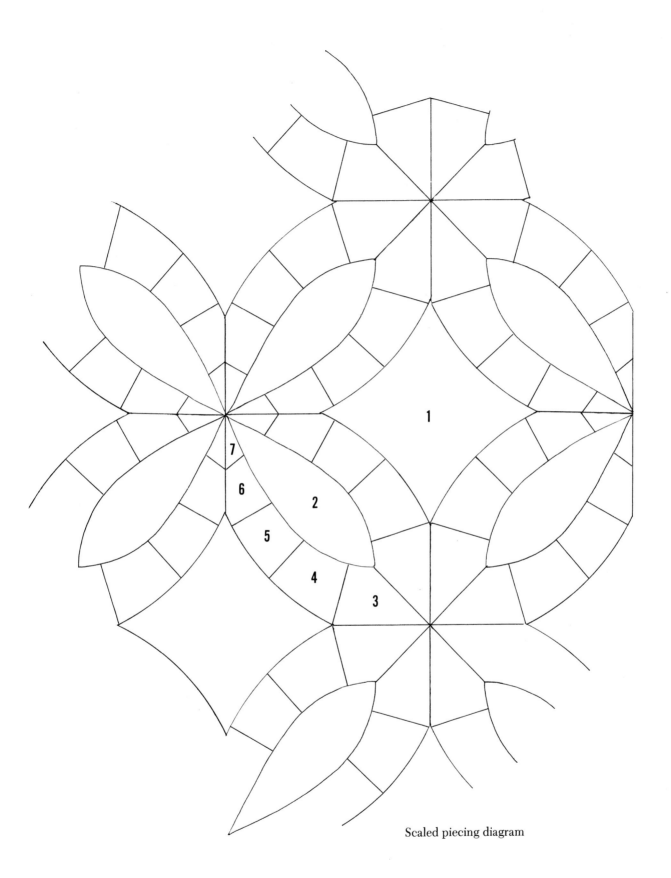

Scaled piecing diagram

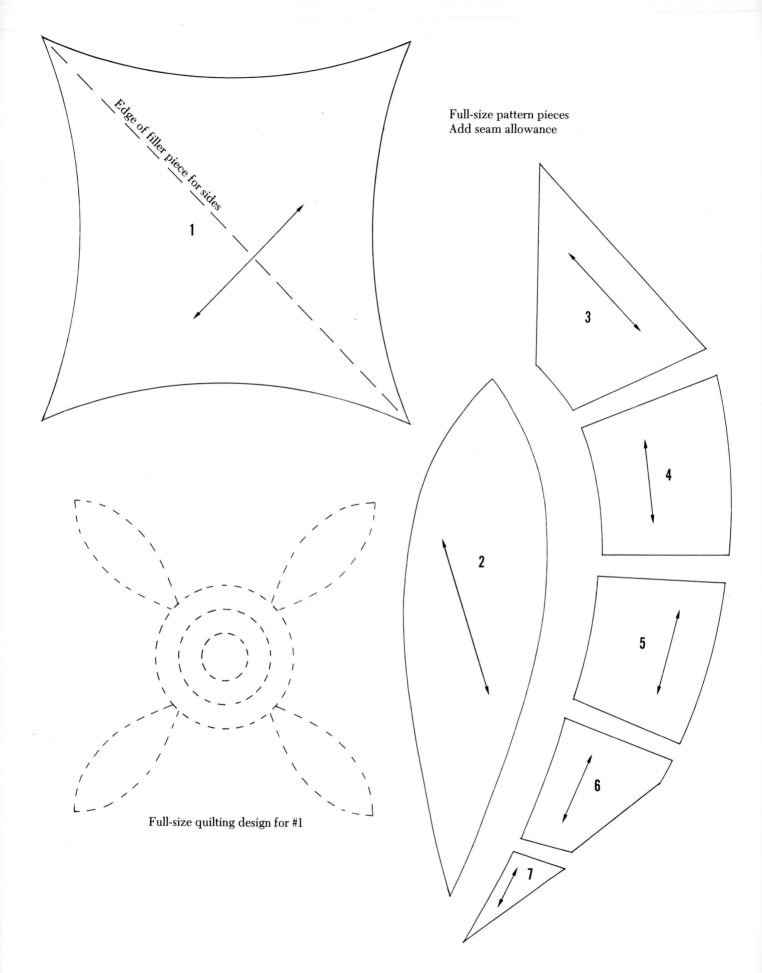

Edge of filler piece for sides

1

Full-size pattern pieces
Add seam allowance

3

4

2

5

6

7

Full-size quilting design for #1

NOTES

1. John Rice Irwin, *A People & Their Quilts* (West Chester, Pa.: Schiffer Publishing, Ltd., 1984), p. 137.

2. Virginia Snow, *Grandma Dexter Appliqué and Patchwork Designs*, Bk. 36 (Elgin, Ill.: Virginia Snow Studios, undated (released in the early 1930s).

3. Irwin, *A People & Their Quilts*, p. 140.

4. Mary Washington Clarke, *Kentucky Quilts and Their Makers* (Lexington, Ky.: The University Press of Kentucky, 1976), p. 5.

5. Irwin, *A People & Their Quilts*, p. 105.

6. Ibid., p. 128.